WHEN THE DOCTOR SAYS, "NO MORE SALT," DON'T THINK BLAND, THINK DELICIOUS!

GLAZED ORANGE BREAD
PIQUANT MEAT SAUCE
APRIL FOOL'S GINGERBREAD
NO-CHEATING CHOCOLATE CAKE
KITCHEN GARDEN DRESSING
CUSTARD-FILLED CREAM PUFFS

These are just some of the many enticing recipes for your favorite delights that can be prepared in a new, healthier way. This unique and informative guide to low sodium cookery will open the door to a zesty eating adventure—and once again you'll be enjoying savory family meals and special treats with all the trimmings. You'll be eating in good taste—and in good health!

"Very fine recipes and good practical advice."

—Santa Barbara
News-Press

SIGNET Books of Special Interest

Living Salt Free and Easy

The First Low Sodium Handbook
with Adapted Recipes for
Old-fashioned Meals and Dessert Treats

by
Anna Houston Thorburn
with Phyllis Turner

A SIGNET BOOK
NEW AMERICAN LIBRARY
TIMES MIRROR

COPYRIGHT © 1975 BY ANNA HOUSTON THORBURN AND
PHYLLIS TURNER

Library of Congress Catalog Card Number: 74-16983

This is an authorized reprint of a hardcover edition published
by Douglas-West Publishers, Inc.

 SIGNET TRADEMARK REG. U.S. PAT. OFF. AND FOREIGN COUNTRIES
REGISTERED TRADEMARK—MARCA REGISTRADA
HECHO EN CHICAGO, U.S.A.

SIGNET, SIGNET CLASSICS, MENTOR, PLUME AND MERIDIAN BOOKS
are published by The New American Library, Inc.,
1301 Avenue of the Americas, New York, New York 10019

FIRST SIGNET PRINTING, SEPTEMBER, 1976

1 2 3 4 5 6 7 8 9

PRINTED IN THE UNITED STATES OF AMERICA

ACKNOWLEDGMENTS

For their professional expertise and encouragement throughout the preparation of this book, my thanks to these members of the staff at Salem Hospital, Salem, Massachusetts:

Associate Cardiologists Dr. Lawrence J. Finkelstein, Dr. Maximiliaan G. Kaulbach, and Dr. John C. Santos, together with their colleagues Dr. Gerard Michaud and Dr. Robert Nangle.

To Miss Janice Pender, therapeutic dietitian, and her associate, Mrs. Jane Henry, whose dual efforts are evident in the Appendix of this book.

Also to my family and many others who shared in the testing of these adapted recipes, my grateful appreciation.

And a very special thanks to my neighbor and collaborator, Phyllis Turner, for patient and expert editorial assistance.

Anna Houston Thorburn,
Marblehead, Mass.

EDITORIAL COMMENT

References to specific brand-name products are not to be construed as commercial
advertising or solicited endorsements. They
were the only available low sodium products in the area and their usage achieved
the best results. Other equally satisfactory
brands of these items may be available in
different parts of the country.

Anna Houston Thorburn

DEDICATION

to
Lewis
whose appetite for
the good things in life
prompted my ventures
into special cookery

Contents

RECIPES

Breads & Muffins

Cakes

Cookies

Pastry and Pies

Puddings

Salad Days

Miscellaneous Marvels

Chapter 1

... The Lord Helps Those ...

The doctor ordered it but he did not have to cook it—or eat it!

I don't know which of us, my husband or I, was more exasperated by that unexpected and irrevocable order. Suddenly the word "no" dominated our daily meals, even our lives.

For several years I had been making a collection of old family recipes, and as a practical hobby as well as being fond of good cooking, I had put most of the collection to everyday use and occasionally at festive gatherings with family and friends. Preparing these traditional dishes for holiday menus soon became a culinary version of an old-fashioned sewing bee; everyone contributed and enjoyed.

Encouraged by their enthusiasm and to some extent by creative curiosity, I had gradually revised each old recipe, adapting it to modern shortcuts while retaining those natural flavors, characteristic of good home cooking, which many contemporary dishes sometimes lack. Successfully updating ancestral recipes which had originated in Scotland, England, and New England required both imagination and culinary skills. To have achieved that objective was a considerable satisfaction to me. And at last they had been organized and in-

1

dexed into time-saving versions, readily at hand for any daily or special occasion.

Then, in 1960, my husband had a series of medical appointments and two sojourns in Salem Hospital at Salem, Massachusetts. Because of seriously high blood pressure, for the rest of his life he was to have no salt, no regular milk, no packaged foods containing sodium whether natural or added, no store-bought muffins, pies, and cakes, no convenient snack foods. Almost overnight my recipe collection had become as obsolete as a horse and carriage on a modern freeway! Every one of those old recipes called for high sodium ingredients.

Soon after the doctor's edict to my husband, I began to notice certain symptoms of my own which, at first, I thought were stubborn "allergic" reactions to repeated use of the hated word "no." We had been given a long list of foods which never were to be served again, and a discouragingly skimpy list of what could be eaten. That is to say, *could* be eaten if one were on the verge of starvation! They were tasteless, bland concoctions which might be endured but rarely, if ever, relished. Such menus when prescribed for a patient in the hospital for a temporary period and under treatment requiring rigidly strict diet might be adhered to with patience. But for someone leading a normal life in every way and working up a hearty appetite suddenly to be faced with meals as monotonous as a baby's formula, it was nothing less than heavy penance. Anyone who is or has been on a low sodium regime will readily attest to this.

To my hopeful inquiries about some of our very favorite foods, the doctor had but one simple response: No! No! No! No more chocolate cake, gingerbread, bakery pies, or other goodies. No more snacks to munch, or midnight helpings of cooling Jell-O on a warm summer night. No more gourmet meals prepared from those treasured old family recipes.

The long list of forbidden fare began to haunt me. Those files of modernized recipes, reposing unused on the kitchen shelf, taunted me.

Main dishes were not at all discouraging, I found, once I memorized the basic restrictions. Only a few meats such as corned beef, ham, frankfurters, and cold cuts were prohibited due to their high sodium content. But because the forbidden fare *was* forbidden my natural stubbornness was challenged. I would find *some way* to restore those delicious foods to our daily meals and to a festive table for company and family gatherings!

"Have you ever *tried* any of this food?" I asked my husband's doctor.

"No, and I hope I never have to," he frankly confessed.

"If one *must* eat such fare, at least it should be possible to *prepare* it with some taste."

He agreed. "What about your collection of recipes, Anna? Could you use low sodium ingredients in some of the pastry recipes and still get the same taste results?"

His question was an inspiration.

"Why not try it?" I responded.

Anything that offered a possible reprieve from a lifetime sentence to bland, tasteless food was certainly worth a trial.

Once I had located the various ingredients which could be substituted—a task that required many weeks of study and research—I was on the way to exciting discoveries. Forbidden dishes were magically changed into permissible ones—not only for my husband and myself but for serving to family members and guests whose food was not restricted, without anyone ever noticing the difference!

Friends, and associates at the hospital where I served as a volunteer, asked for copies of my adapted recipes. Later I was invited to demonstrate their preparation on closed circuit television for the benefit of the hospital personnel and patients.

Happily, to any dreary chant, "I can't have . . . ," I was now able to say, "you certainly can *if* it is prepared properly."

Inevitably, the complete answer to questions and requests was a book.

What is presented here is more than a cookbook. It is the first specific guide to shopping for doctor-approved low sodium foods and preparing salt-free tasty old-fashioned dishes made from recipes adapted to that purpose. It also includes a sizable collection of recipes for a wide variety of desserts, salads, hot breads, snacks, and party fare. A whole section is devoted to quick main dishes prepared from low sodium canned goods.

Preparing these low sodium meals can become a real adventure in special cookery. All you need do is to follow the simplified directions, read labels carefully when you go shopping to make sure the ingredients are right, then start cooking! Soon you will again be enjoying delicious family meals and serving those special treats "with all the trimmings" at social gatherings, without jeopardy to health and well-being.

Chapter 2

... In the Beginning ...

The doctor's suggestion was all the encouragement needed to stir my creative senses. I set about the optimistic task with practical determination. Certainly, I reasoned, if there were *some* substitutes for the everyday foods on that forbidden list, there must be many others.

The first step, of course, was to learn more about the culprit that was contributing to my husband's health problem—high sodium foods. Salt, as a condiment, and foods high in sodium, are a significant part of the average family's meals. According to the best medical authorities, these contribute significantly to major health problems such as high blood pressure.

Many people avoid salt for various medical reasons. But a salt-free diet is *not* the same as a low sodium regime for the preparation of meals. *Salt-free* refers to the restriction of but one form of sodium, albeit a potent one. Table salt is approximately 40 percent sodium and, as I soon discovered, there are 2300 milligrams of sodium in *one* teaspoon of salt. And that equals 2.3 grams, if you're counting grams, too! Why was that much sodium a menace? My nonprofessional answer, arrived at through research and asking questions of experts, proved authentic and quite simple.

Among other contributions to the functioning of the

human body, sodium causes the tissues to retain fluid. This, to a degree, is beneficial. But faulty mechanism or imbalance due to other causes may permit too much retention. Then the whole system has to work harder to control it. Cutting down on sodium intake restores a more normal balance, thus allowing the entire system to function with less strain. For example, compare the human body to an automobile's engine. A car needs brakes, but it will not perform efficiently if driven with the emergency brake on. High sodium content in many foods tends to act as a brake against normal bodily functioning.

Surprisingly, I discovered that there are over 23 million Americans with hypertension (high blood pressure), and it is estimated that less than half of these are aware of the condition or its dangers. Only a physician, of course, can advise the specific degree of sodium restriction for each individual. A number of tests are required to determine this and no two cases are alike. If you are in doubt about acceptable foods for this or any other health condition, consult your doctor. Do *not* take the advice of a neighbor or acquaintance who may claim to have had "the same problem."

Fortunately, in our research, we had access to the Salem Hospital medical library and fairly frequent opportunity to consult with staff doctors. We also had access to the city's public libraries which provided practical information on various health problems: diet therapy, food analyses, and a hundred other pieces of knowledge on subjects that a few months earlier would not have engaged my attention at all.

Sodium is found in almost all foodstuffs and liquids, even our drinking water. It is also present in many of the items in the home medicine chest: a number of headache remedies, laxatives, antacids, and cough drops contain surprisingly high amounts of sodium. Many do not, but be sure to ask your doctor which ones you should use. It is *not* a frivolous question.

Methods for measuring exact amounts of sodium in foods are still not completely standardized, but we do know which edibles are to be avoided because of high sodium content and which, happily, are low in natural sodium. For the present, all charts regarding sodium content should be considered approximate; a milligram or two does not make a significant difference. Beets, celery, spinach, and shellfish (but not fresh fish, even when taken from the salty ocean) are examples of foods that are high in natural sodium whether processed or cooked. Most of us know that table salt is sodium chloride, and that a package of baking soda is labeled sodium bicarbonate. What was puzzling was that if fresh celery or spinach or several other common vegetables were cooked in plain water or by steaming, they still were not permitted on an "approved" list. The reason, of course, was their naturally high sodium content, which was unchanged by cooking.

Once I had a working knowledge of the effects of sodium on the human system, I became interested in learning more about potassium, which was listed in many of the food analyses I had read. Was it a "good" ingredient, or another of those to be regarded with suspicion? Again, research told me that it was, indeed, one of the protective elements. Foods that are high in potassium are important to low sodium regimes for the reason that these two elements, potassium and sodium, are linked together to maintain normal functioning of the body. When we are required to reduce the sodium intake level, the potassium, which should *not* be reduced, is likely to be affected also, thus causing imbalance. Fortunately it is easy to restore and maintain the potassium level. For most practical purposes, it is sufficient to know that potassium is one of the "good guys" in our foods, while sodium in excess becomes one of the "bad guys" in normal human diets.

Many everyday food items contain this valuable element, potassium: bananas, figs, cherries (but not Maraschino cherries—high in sodium), apricots, broccoli, cauliflower, corn, Hershey brand cocoa, non-instant oatmeal, and light table wines. All fruits, of course, should be fresh, sun-dried, or salt-free canned. Vegetables fresh, frozen without salt, or canned with low sodium or salt-free labels. (Specific packaged foods are dealt with at length in Chapter 4; permissible fresh fruits and vegetables are listed with the salad recipes.) If your doctor tells you to "eat a banana every day," he is probably asking you to increase your potassium intake. While bananas are one of the most palatable and accessible foods high in potassium, few of us would want to eat one every day, year round. Therefore, the potassium content of each recipe in this book is given for easy reference in the Appendix.

After weeks of research and consultations with a number of doctors I was ready to embark on the main project: adapting those family recipes to low sodium cookery. It was easy enough to substitute salt-free margarine, low sodium milk, and polyunsaturated oil for the ingredients previously used, but leavening was another matter. I had never used potassium bicarbonate instead of baking soda, nor did I know what to use when an equivalent for baking powder was needed. Moreover, I had not the faintest idea how the substitution of such items was going to affect my recipes.

It was with great trepidation that, after a series of baking tests, I served some of the adapted recipes to family and friends at a weekend gathering. My husband and I had conspired to say nothing about the changes, or my project "operation substitution." To our delight, nobody noticed any alteration in taste or texture. One cousin, who is an excellent cook, remarked, "I just don't know how you do it, Anna! *I'm* never able to get muffins as light as these."

The truth of the matter was that the muffins I served that day *were* lighter—as were all my cakes and pastries prepared with the same substitute ingredients. So successful were these alternatives, I was perfectly happy never to go back to the original high sodium ingredients specified in the old recipes, even had I been permitted to do so. Aside from that, I had discovered a new game which I call Sodium-Saving, for which I drew up the comparison chart on page 10 from a few basic ingredients available in both regular and low sodium forms. Even the hospital doctors were astonished by the sodium-saving accomplished from *adapting*, not prohibiting, favorite recipes and menus.

While this chart lists but a few of the foods available in low sodium form, it graphically indicates how to select alternate ingredients for low sodium meals without sacrificing nutrition or flavor—instead, actually enhancing both. Furthermore, by keeping the sodium intake low wherever possible with other items on the menu, you have more leeway in the choice of meat you serve. Meats are fairly high in natural sodium, but they also provide concentrated quantities of protein, amino acids, iron, and calcium, all vital to general health. In other words, you merely *exchange* high sodium ingredients for others of equal or improved quality in low sodium form—a kind of culinary musical-chairs idea.

Following this general plan, I found that the scores of food items and recipe ingredients now became absorbingly interesting. Discovering new and varied kinds of substitutes which created taste-tempting results became a kind of game which I pursued with

COMPARISON CHART

(mg. means milligrams of sodium)

Low Sodium Item

Baking powder*	1 tsp.	1 mg.
Potassium bicarbonate	1 tsp.	0 mg.
Low sodium milk	1 qt.	25-50 mg.**
Hershey's cocoa	1 tsp.	0 mg.
Salt-free margarine	1 tsp.	1 mg.
Lemon juice	1 tsp.	0 mg.
Corn flakes	1 cup	2 mg.
Catsup	1 tbsp.	0 mg.
Peanut butter	1 tbsp.	7 mg.

Regular Item

Baking powder	1 tsp.	408 mg.
Baking soda	1 tsp.	1232 mg.
All dairy milk	1 qt.	500 mg.
Dutch-process cocoa	1 tsp.	17 mg.
Salted margarine	1 tsp.	55 mg.
Table salt	1 tsp.	2300 mg.
Corn flakes	1 cup	165 mg.
Catsup	1 tbsp.	177 mg.
Peanut butter	1 tbsp.	97 mg.

*Low sodium baking powder formula, to be made up by druggist:

Cornstarch	56.0 grams
Tartaric acid	15.0 grams
Potassium bicarbonate	79.5 grams
Potassium bitartrate	112.25 grams

**Milligrams depend on amount of water used in reconstituting the powdered milk.

enthusiasm. Perhaps you have discovered some of these yourself, but in the event you haven't let me pass on some of the information I found helpful:

Low Sodium Baking Powder: This can be purchased ready-mixed at some supermarkets, or you may have the formula given below the comparison chart made up by your druggist. At first, I thought this might become quite costly, for I was usually cooking up a storm trying out various ways to adapt more of my family recipes. But each jar of low sodium baking powder lasted a surprisingly long time under the circumstances and I kept reminding myself that I was actually saving 408 milligrams of sodium per teaspoon. Also, the foods prepared with it were better tasting and kept fresh longer.

(One small word of warning: If you are converting some of your own favorite recipes to low sodium cookery, be sure to increase the amount of *low sodium baking powder* used by one-half. See Chapter 8, Adapting Your Own Recipes, for more detailed information.)

Keep in mind, however, that all recipes in this book *have been adapted.* Do *not* increase or diminish the amounts listed for any basic ingredients.

Potassium Bicarbonate: This should be used in place of store-bought baking soda, which of course is *sodium* bicarbonate and therefore to be avoided. Potassium bicarbonate is available at most drugstores and may be used in the same amount as regular baking soda. Since it tends to harden in damp weather be sure to keep it in a dry place and tightly covered. If it *does* harden, simply spoon-scrape the amount needed for a recipe.

Milk and Cream: Milk in all forms is naturally high in sodium—whole, skim, low-fat, certified, evaporated, condensed, and powdered. However, the special process used to produce low sodium milk powder greatly reduces the sodium content. At least two brands of this are now available nationally. Personally, I prefer *Featherweight Skim,* made by the Cellu company which also produces other low sodium products you will find listed in the Market Basket chapter. *Lonolac* is equally low in sodium, but is a powdered whole (not skim) milk and higher in calories. It is available at drugstores and can be reconstituted for use in the same manner as *Featherweight Skim*, which was used in adapting the recipes presented here.

Cream, surprisingly, is not a sodium culprit. Any laboratory can precisely separate cream from barn-fresh milk, and analyze every vitamin and mineral element. But the cow already has contributed the neatest trick—keeping all but a fraction of sodium out of the cream! There are only seven milligrams of sodium per tablespoon of cream, which makes it quite permissible for coffee, dessert toppings, and sauces, and on cereals, diluted with water if you prefer. But—*and please note well*—cream substitutes are definitely off-limits. Do not be alarmed by the listing of sodium alginate on cream containers. It is only 1/10th of 1 percent and is used as a preservative for fresh cream.

Chocolate: This is one of the luxuries of cooking, although inadvisable for regular consumption for various reasons ranging from teen-age complexion problems to cranky gall bladders. And it is normally high in sodium content. Hershey brand cocoa is quite another story. It is a safe and elegant answer to the "chocolate" ingredient specified in so many dessert recipes. It may look sinfully like authentic Dutch-process chocolate (as in Kay's No-Cheating Chocolate Cake recipe on page 78) and produce a cake as dark, rich, and moist as the best devil's food, but it is definitely approved for low sodium cooking. This cocoa may also be used in cookies, puddings, sauces, gelatins —in fact, any recipe that calls for the use of chocolate.

As an old-fashioned treat on chilly evenings, my husband and I like nothing better than *Chocolat au Crème*, which is a pot of cocoa made stronger than the directions on the Hershey box indicate. I use Featherweight Skim milk, vanilla sugar (see recipe, page 115), and a touch of coffee in the mixture. If doctor-approved, a splash of good brandy is a festive addition. Top each cup or mug with flavored whipped cream. Swiss yodeling may come naturally after the first few sips!

Salt-Free Margarine: For this, my choice is Fleischmann's brand. It is made with pure corn oil and has fewer additives than others. You will find its green-wrapped package in the freezer section of most supermarkets. It should be kept frozen, except for the ¼-pound stick you are currently using. If your doctor permits butter in spite of its saturated fat content, you can also find salt-free sweet butter in the store's freezer area. Be sure to read the label and choose a brand which has the purest ingredients.

Salt Substitutes: Several brands are now available in the diet sections of supermarkets. However, some physicians do not approve of these and it would be wise to ask your doctor about them. My husband prefers to substitute lemon juice. For him all salt substitutes have a brackish taste. But some of our friends who use them have no complaints at all. Whatever your choice, I do not recommend them in cooking.

The much-advertised "low salt" is entirely inadvisable since it still has half the sodium content of regular salt, about 1150 mg. of sodium per teaspoon! You can easily approximate a salty flavor in your cooking with lemon juice, herbs, vinegar, or dry table wines.

Cereals: A variety of these now are packaged for low sodium breakfasts, and several of these are listed in Chapter 4, The Shopping List. Some of the so-called "back to nature" cereals are not recommended since they contain salt as well as sodium-tinged ingredients. At least one brand in this category has only minimal nutritional value, despite the "wholesome" advertising; and most are overpriced considering their low food value. The exceptions, for me at least, which are listed in the Shopping List chapter are two granolas. Or, you may prefer to make your own budget-minded "granola" by combining puffed rice, puffed wheat, *light* brown sugar, wheat germ, chopped unsalted nuts, and sun-dried diced fruits. It may be prepared in quantity and stored in the refrigerator, tightly covered, ready for serving. Children and adults usually enjoy this and it is more nutritious than most packaged cereals on the grocer's shelves. Give it a family name, if you wish, chosen by the children. It makes good eating for snack times as well as breakfast or brunch.

Bacon Substitute: Who can resist the unique aroma of bacon gently frying to a delicate crispness? Although regular bacon is forbidden in low sodium cookery, Bakon Yeast restores the flavor to scrambled eggs, cornbread, and casserole dishes. It is a hickory-smoked yeast powder which you can sprinkle on or mix into any recipe you wish to give that robust zest. Bakon Yeast is available at health food stores and some supermarkets.

Syrups: Gingerbread was one of our favorite desserts and I stopped making it because I could no longer use molasses, which is high in sodium. My ultimate answer to this restriction was April Fool's Gingerbread (recipe on page 74) in which no molasses is used but the same memorable flavor is achieved successfully.

Syrups that are pure natural products and contain no soda preservatives or sodium are entirely acceptable. If you have been using maple-*flavored* syrup you now have a good reason to indulge in real maple syrup itself, although it is a little more expensive. Syrups in which fruits are canned are acceptable as long as they do not contain sodium preservatives (which would be listed on the labels), and these make delectable toppings for custards, breakfast breads, and dessert pancakes. Pure honey, just as the bees produced it, is a boon to special menus. And this natural food is available in an assortment of subtle flavors by the simple process of the bees' diet being restricted to a single variety of blossom! Our introduction to this was a gift-box from California which contained ten small jars, each with a different flavored honey.

Try making your own economical syrups, experimenting with proportions until they suit your fancy. One basic recipe: 2 ounces honey, 2 ounces pure maple syrup, 2 teaspoons cornstarch or arrowroot, and 1 cup cold water. Stir well in a saucepan and heat to a simmer until it thickens. This is delicious, hot or cold, and can be varied by adding a dash of rum or brandy (or extracts of these) as a dessert topping.

Condiments: Manufacturers of items in this category have dealt kindly with low sodium requirements. Many of those most commonly used come in low sodium forms and are available in the diet sections of supermarkets as well as health food stores. Catsup, chili sauce, prepared mustard, and a few less common items bear the low sodium label, as you will discern from the Shopping List chapter. You can make your own *Sauce Maison* by combining different measuring-spoon amounts of the first four named items and adding a little sugar. It is a savory accompaniment for steak, hamburgers, broiled fish, roasts, and may be added to sandwich fillings.

Peanut Butter: This favorite of all ages is available in two reliable low sodium brands (see page 27); both come only in the smooth-style spread. If you prefer the chunky variety, simply mix in a portion of chopped *unsalted* peanuts for added texture and protein.

We have dealt more fully with many varieties of acceptable foods and their accompaniments in later chapters. But here is a good place to remind you that "substitutes" in this situation are in no sense imitations of inferior quality. Rather, we simply *exchange* a high sodium ingredient for a better or more imaginative low sodium one, thereby producing meals for the whole family and your guests, not "diet food" for one individual.

Chapter 3

... *The Market Basket* ...

During a period of several months while assembling information on low sodium products and preparing reliable listings on commercial items most frequently used, we acquired a great many pamphlets and advertising brochures which were carefully studied. Therefore all products mentioned in this chapter are items we have tested and personally endorse.

However, these are personal preferences, not strictly commercial endorsements. Similar products, not immediately available in our neighborhood, may be equally satisfactory. Many new products are now being introduced as low sodium cookery becomes more widely recognized as a reliable health guard.

Items most frequently used in quantity—canned goods and low sodium milk powder—may be purchased by the case. That is, if you have sufficient storage space. But if you are just beginning this venture into low sodium cookery it is best to purchase a can or a package of such items at a time until you are sure you like the product; then perhaps buy mixed cases of canned vegetables and fruits—which most markets will sell at discounts—and packaged foods in half-dozen lots for convenience and sizable savings.

Patronizing a store which carries a large selection of low sodium products has advantages. It encourages the management to stock more such items and to arrange for special orders if required; and as the demand for low sodium products increases in your community customers are assured of plentiful stocks and varieties.

Almost any local independent bakery can easily be persuaded to provide low sodium breads if assured of regular sales. Give him that assurance by placing your order weekly or buying in quantity for home freezing. As the news spreads through the neighborhood you can be sure of steady supply. Preparing a batch of water-based salt-free dough (using any kind of flour except dark rye or self-rising) is relatively easy for the baker. Variety may be added to the low sodium quality by taste-boosters such as caraway, poppy, or sesame seeds and sun-dried raisins, mixed into the dough or sprinkled on top before baking. Adding onion flakes to salt-free sourdough bread makes an excellent item for family or company serving.

Since low sodium breads contain no preservatives they must be kept in the freezer section of your refrigerator to remain fresh for longer than a few days. A loaf or two in current use should be kept in the refrigerator between servings. A few commercial brands of low sodium bread are acceptable and quite satisfactory. A loaf or two of these may be kept on hand in the freezer in case you run out of home-baked breads before your regular baking days. Just make sure the brand you buy is salt-free and water-based, not milk-based. All "quick breads"—those made with baking soda and regular baking powder—should be avoided. However, you can make such breads yourself by using one of the adapted recipes provided in the recipe section. All ingredients listed are of low sodium content.

Distribution of commercial low sodium products in some sections of the country is still a problem. Local stores and supermarkets may not stock such items at all, particularly those stores near camping grounds and other vacation facilities. We found this the case with the only market near our summer camp in New Hampshire. They carried low sodium canned goods but did not stock the powdered low sodium milk put out by the same manufacturer. Demand in these isolated areas is limited since the population fluctuates seasonally. Also, a new product that is being "spot-tested" may be sold only in selected areas for a year or more before being given national distribution.

The market list provided in Chapter 4 is designed to give you general information on a variety of low sodium products, and to suggest alternative brand names wherever possible. Health food stores are rapidly becoming a part of most communities. Many of these are well stocked with low sodium products; others concentrate on vitamin food supplements and organically grown fruits and vegetables. (Check the yellow pages of your telephone book for location of such stores. Find out what products suitable to your regime are available.) Large department stores frequently have sections devoted to gourmet foods and specialty items. Many drugstores are now veritable shopping centers which may carry such items. Certainly among these various outlets you are sure to find a wide variety of low sodium products in your own neighborhood. Some of these items also may be manufactured in your community. Consumer action and some voluntary participation by commercial processors now have made mandatory information-labeling on over 60 percent of packaged foods.

Low sodium packaged foods are now labeled in various ways, using such phrases as *salt-controlled,* *salt-reduced,* as well as salt-free and low sodium designations. Basically these tend to mean the same thing. Some labels also give the milligrams of sodium in the package; but be sure to read the fine print on such labels and avoid any product that lists as ingredients salt, sodium, MSG (monosodium glutamate), leavening, soda, milk, milk powder, non-fat milk solids, and all preservatives that contain sodium. There is one exception: plain, *not* pre-whipped, cream where the sodium alginate is negligible, insufficient for concern. Ascorbic acid, frequently used as a preservative in fresh fruits and juices, is harmless.

Once you have become a confirmed label reader you will find that many regular brand canned goods and packaged and frozen vegetables and fruits are prepared without salt or sodium preservatives. (See Salad Fruits, Vegetables, & Greens section.) If the ingredients of can or package are not listed on the label it might be best to bypass the product at least until you are better informed about its contents. The fact that it may be displayed on the diet section shelves does not mean it is of low sodium content. A great many products in that department may be for reducing, diabetic, or allergy diets, and could contain ingredients not suitable to low sodium regimes. Some items labeled as low sodium may still contain too much sodium for your particular use. For instance, sodium may be listed by milligrams and grams (mg. and gr.) per serving, or based on total contents, such as 3.4 mg. per ounce. Choose the one with lowest sodium count.

Cheese is high in natural sodium, and therefore is not recommended. Low sodium cottage cheese is bland but can be made quite appetizing by the addition of chopped low sodium pickles, minced onion and green peppers, or diced fruit.

You will find hundreds of products in your neighborhood stores and supermarkets from which to choose. Start learning to read and understand labels; then make your own taste tests. Keep a record of the brand names you like and find suitable, where you purchased them, and other helpful reminders. Attaching the labels to your notebook may help to simplify your marketing.

NOTE: Some physicians and hospital dietitians provide patients with food charts which list grams rather than milligrams. However, the majority of commercial products list sodium in milligrams on package labels; therefore we have followed that method throughout this book. No complicated arithmetic is involved: 1 gram equals 1000 milligrams.

Chapter 4

... The Shopping List ...

Unless a specific manufacturer's name is given for the items listed here, any regular brand of the product may be used so long as its label indicates *complete* ingredients. Avoid all foods high in natural sodium.

BEVERAGES

Coffee
    Bean, ground, freeze-dried, powdered
Sanka and Postum
Tea
    Leaves, bags, instant
Cocoa
    Hershey's plain, not with milk powder
Juice
    All fresh or bottled and frozen without sodium preservative
With Doctor's Permission
    Gin, vodka, whiskey, vermouth, light table wines, but not cooking sherry. Champagne, anyone?
Mixers
    Club soda, water. Ask doctor about others.

Milk

> Low sodium powdered, reconstituted. Regular whole or skim milk *only* with doctor's permission.

BREAD, CRACKERS

Low sodium white bread
> Kazanoff

Salt-free gluten bread
> Estee

Local bakery
> See page 18

Melba toast: white, rye, wheat
> Old London by Borden's

Wheat wafers
> Venus

Waldorf crackers
> Keebler

Matzoh, plain or Passover

CEREALS

Puffed wheat, plain
Puffed rice, plain
Shredded wheat biscuits
Low sodium corn flakes
> Cellu Featherweight and other brands

Familia granola
> Swiss Import

Toasted oats granola
> Cellu Featherweight

Non-instant oatmeal
Non-instant Cream of Wheat
Wheat germ

CONDIMENTS

Chili Sauce, low sodium ⎫ Chicago Dietetic
Tomato Paste, low sodium ⎪ Supply, distributed
Catsup, low sodium ⎬ under the Cellu
Salad Mustard, low sodium ⎪ Featherweight
Pickles, Relish, low sodium ⎭ label
Salt Substitute
    Various brands, but not Morton's Lite Salt
ReaLemon
    Reconstituted lemon juice by Borden's

DAIRY, SHORTENING

Low Sodium Skim Milk Powder
    Cellu Featherweight
Low Sodium Whole Milk Powder
    Lonolac (at drugstore)
Cream, fresh only
Salt-Free Margarine
    In freezer case in market
Unsalted Sweet Butter
    In freezer case in market
Vegetable Shortening
    Crisco, Spry, etc.
Pam Spray-On Vegetable Coating
    Boyle-Midway
Polyunsaturated Oils

ENTREES

Lamb, Beef, and Chicken Stews
    Cellu Featherweight

Spanish Rice
    Cellu Featherweight
Beef Stew
    Claybourne

FISH

Tuna
    Chicken of the Sea Diet Pack and Feather-
    weight
Salmon
    S & W "for salt-controlled diets," Cellu
    Featherweight
Shrimp (occasional treat)
    Cellu Featherweight

GELATINS

Cherry, Lime, Orange, Raspberry, Lemon
    D-Zerta low sodium label, Cellu Feather-
    weight

HERBS, SPICES
See page 30

SOUPS

Condensed
    Cream of Mushroom ⎫
    Chicken Noodle   ⎪
    Tomato   ⎬ Cellu Featherweight
    Tomato with Rice   ⎪
    Beef and Chicken   ⎪
    Bouillon Cubes   ⎭

Ready to Serve
Green Pea ⎫
Tomato ⎬ Campbell's low sodium
Vegetable ⎭ label
Vegetable Beef

SWEETENERS

Sugar
White, light brown
Honey
Pure Maple Syrup
Pure Jellies, Jams
Sugar Substitutes
Ask doctor

TV SNACKS

Salt-Free Peanuts
Planter's
Peanuts in Shells
3 Marshmallows
10 Jelly Beans
2 Large or 16 Small Gum Drops
Hard Candy—barley sugar type
Chewing Gum
Bread Sticks ⎫
Kichels ⎬ Stella D'Oro low sodium
Peach-Apricot Pastry ⎭
No-Salt Potato Sticks
Capitol Charter
No-Salt Potato Chips
Vincent's

VEGETABLES

Asparagus Tips
Cream-Style Corn
Whole-Kernel Corn } Cellu Featherweight
Cut Green Beans
Sweet Peas

Asparagus
Golden Corn } S & W salt-controlled diet
Mixed Vegetables } label
Tomatoes
    S & W salt-controlled diet label
    Diet Delight reduced-salt diet label

For other vegetables such as frozen or canned squash, green beans, asparagus, broccoli, pumpkin, plain onions, or any item not naturally high in sodium or packed in a sauce mixture, *read the label!*

MISCELLANEOUS

Peanut Butter
    Peter Pan low sodium, Cellu Featherweight
Bakon Yeast
    Bakon Yeast, Inc.
Cocoa
    Hershey's
Low Sodium Baking Powder
    See formula on page 10, or Cellu Feather-
    weight
Baking Soda Alternative
    Potassium bicarbonate, drugstore

Chapter 5

... Larded with Sweet Flowers ...

Ancient volumes which were called Herbals and dealt with the use of edible leaves, seeds, and blossoms, predate the time of Shakespeare. There are early Greek and Roman scrolls devoted to the subject, while the Bard's writings have frequent references such as "larded with sweet flowers" and "rosemary for remembrance."

When I first began learning to cook there were less than a dozen kinds of seasoning herbs, spices, and extracts on grocers' shelves. Today the variety of such items is so extensive that it would astonish Marco Polo, that historical figure who centuries ago searched the then uncharted world for even a few of these. Fortunes were spent in the spice trades but now the cost to modern cooks is negligible considering the pure magic of these flavor enhancers. Almost every family cook knows that "a sprinkle of this and a dash of that" often can transform an ordinary dish into a gourmet's delight.

Only a few flavorings should be avoided when preparing low sodium meals. Obviously *seasoning salts* are among these: celery, onion, and garlic. Nor should you use unidentified mixtures, *dried* parsley, or, in fact, anything that is not on the Herb and Spice Table at the end of this chapter. All items listed have been analyzed at one milligram or less per teaspoon; and only a party-sized recipe would require that amount.

The kind and amount of herbs, spices, or flavoring used in any recipe is, to some degree, the choice of the cook. One may use basil to enliven the taste of noodles; another prefers oregano. Still another might use a little of both. Subtle seasoning is what makes each cook's dishes unique. Measurements should be flexible, starting with a minimum amount and adding more as desired. Dried herbs and spices are likely to be stronger than the fresh variety. It is well to keep in mind also that taste buds which have been numbed for years by table salt may require at least a few weeks to revive. Amounts of seasoning or flavoring may need to be adjusted as favorite recipes are repeated.

If you are a house-plant enthusiast, an indoor herb garden can be a delightful undertaking. Many herbs are for sale in large commercial greenhouses and florist shops and it is better to get the plants already started than to grow them from seed. Herbs should have filtered sunlight about half the day and be kept as cool as possible. Among the easier ones to maintain are parsley, sweet basil, chives, rosemary, garden sage, and winter savory.

For those not accustomed to using a variety of herbs and spices but who want to start enlivening family meals and party fare, it is best to check the qualities of unfamiliar items before using them. For instance, if you like the taste of licorice you will enjoy anise. If not, you will ruin a recipe. Test characteristics before using. Several reliable, informative books on herbs and spices are available in inexpensive paperback editions, and at your public library. You are sure to find that testing selected seasonings will relieve the monotony of preparing "just another meal," especially a low sodium one.

The following herbs and spices most frequently used by gourmet cooks, and which are permissible in low sodium regimes, will get you off to the right start with your own culinary adventures:

SPICES AND HERBS

Allspice
Anise Seed
Apple Pie Spice
Basil
Bay Leaf
Bell's Seasoning
Caraway Seed
Cardamom
Cassia
Chervil
Chili Con Carne
    Seasoning
Chili Pequin
    (not powder)
Chives
Cinnamon
Clove

Coriander
Cumin
Curry
Dill, seed or fresh
Fennel
Fenugreek
Fines Herbes
Garlic Powder
Ginger
Gumbo Filé
Horseradish, fresh
Juniper Berry
Mace
Marjoram
Mint
Mustard, dry or low
    sodium brand

Nutmeg
Onion Flakes
Oregano
Parsley, fresh
Pepper
Pickling Spice
Poppy Seed
Rosemary
Saffron
Sage
Salad Herbs
Savory
Shallot
Tarragon
Thyme
Turmeric

Extracts

| Almond | Banana | Lemon | Onion | Peppermint |
| Anise | Brandy | Maple | Orange | Rum |

(Although not categorized as flavoring extracts, bottled grated lemon and orange rind are usually available at well-stocked food stores. They may be more convenient than grating your own, but they also may be more expensive.)

Chapter 6

...Lazy Day Meals...

For those just home from the hospital, or who have suddenly been given the "no salt, low sodium" order by their doctors, the first weeks of meal planning can become quite depressing. The chances are, you will be just plain scared—afraid to serve anything that isn't on the list provided by the doctor or dietitian—and the main ingredients in any meal you prepare are likely to be more "terror" and "will power," not in the least appetizing by normally accepted standards.

This is the ideal time to serve the "extra goodies" to which our recipe section is devoted. Concentrate on the easy ones listed in Chapter 7. So that you do not feel chained to the stove, take advantage of low sodium canned goods for your main dishes. It will be helpful to have menu ideas for quick preparation while you are trying out the recipes for desserts and hot breads, cookies and snacks.

The following menus—a whole week's worth of main dishes—should get you through those first weeks without anxiety. Exact proportions and seasonings are flexible to some extent, governed only by low sodium ingredients and the cook's preferences in seasonings. Use any of the herbs and spices listed on page 30, and any vegetables listed on page 103 if your own preferences are not included in these menu suggestions.

Later, you will be able to create your own "lazy day" meals for impromptu serving.

Each recipe provides generous servings for two. Use of these commercial low sodium salt-controlled products will give you more freedom in the choices of meat and fish you prepare, and more time to make the hot breads and other treats for which recipes are provided in other chapters.

QUICK MENUS

— 1 —

Add low sodium catsup, dried onion flakes, and a pinch of thyme to the contents of 1 can S & W brand (labeled "for salt-controlled diets") lamb stew. Fill small hollowed-out green peppers with mixture, top with a sprinkling of wheat germ. Bake in a pie plate with ½ inch water until done. Serve with canned S & W salt-controlled whole-kernel or cream-style corn (Cellu Featherweight makes this too) and fresh sliced mushrooms sautéed in a skillet with corn oil, lemon juice, and fresh-ground pepper. Add low sodium bread sticks by Stella d'Oro.

— 2 —

Combine cooked elbow macaroni with pan-browned lean hamburger. Add 1 can low sodium tomatoes (see Chapter 4 for brands), cut up, with juice. Top with wheat germ and bake until bubbly. Add water and lemon juice during cooking if mixture becomes too dry. Serve with low sodium canned peas heated up with a pinch of sweet basil and about a teaspoon of chopped scallion or dried minced onion.

— 3 —

Combine contents of 1 can Featherweight low sodium
cream of mushroom soup, 1 can same brand salmon,
flaked, 1 can S & W salt-controlled peas or green beans,
a generous squeeze of lemon, and a pinch of any
favorite herb such as chervil or sage. Heat in double
boiler. Serve in halved Popovers (recipe on page 73),
or on toasted low sodium bread or a nest of low
sodium potato sticks. Accompany this with a Waldorf
salad made with cut up fresh apple, lemon juice,
chopped unsalted walnuts, lettuce, and Aunt Emma's
Boil-Up Dressing (recipe on page 106).

— 4 —

Combine 1 can Chicken of the Sea low sodium label
tuna, cooked thin noodles, dill (seed or fresh
chopped), 1 can Featherweight brand low sodium
cream of mushroom soup. Bake in individual Pam-
sprayed casseroles topped with low sodium canned
asparagus tips dotted with salt-free margarine or unsalted butter, a sprinkling of wheat germ, and a dash
of lemon juice. This is attractive garnished with strips
of canned pimiento, too. Serve with any combination
of fruits, greens, and dressings in the Salad Days
recipe section (see page 103).

— 5 —

Cook Minute Rice according to directions, omitting
salt and using canned Featherweight low sodium
chicken broth (or same brand dissolved bouillon cube)
instead of water. Add about ½ teaspoon curry powder
to the broth before cooking rice in it. In a separate
pan, add leftover diced chicken or turkey white meat,
diced green pepper, and pimiento to 1 can Featherweight cream of mushroom soup. A dash of good dry

sherry (not cooking sherry) is a nice addition. Now, you can either combine all of this with cooked rice and bake it in a casserole, or heat the creamed mixture in a double boiler and serve it on top of the fluffed rice. For a more oriental flavor, add ¼ cup sun-dried raisins to the rice before cooking and be more generous with the curry powder. Serve with broiled slices of canned pineapple and a currant jelly to which you have added a diced slice of melon.

— 6 —

Bake lean pork chops or skinned chicken breasts in a creole sauce made with thin-sliced onion, green pepper, and the contents of 1 can low sodium peeled tomatoes, diced, with juice, and some low sodium catsup or low sodium chili sauce. Serve with baked scalloped potatoes which have been prepared with Campbell's ready-to-serve (not condensed) low sodium cream of mushroom soup or low sodium reconstituted milk with plenty of chopped chives or sweet onions, grated pepper, and a sprinkling of Bakon Yeast. The Double Duty Corn Bread recipe on page 69 is excellent served with this main course.

— 7 —

For a man-hearty soup, sauté onion, dried oregano, and green pepper in a bit of corn oil. Add to a large saucepan in which you have put 1 can low sodium tomatoes, cut up, with the juice, 1 can Campbell's low sodium brand vegetable soup, 1 can S & W salt-controlled brand whole-kernel corn, undrained, and about ½ cup okra. Add any leftover cooked diced lamb, beef, or poultry or cooked fresh fish, flaked. Bring to a boil while stirring; add water if necessary. Try serving this with a salad of sliced cucumber, quartered hard-cooked egg, halved seedless grapes, and watercress, topped with Hester's French-Style Dressing. The recipe is on page 106.

The great taste of any really thick, chunky soup comes from all the inexpensive variations which often provide uses for bits of leftovers. If you like a hot, pungent flavor, sprinkle with cayenne pepper or add gumbo filé just before serving. If the soup is mostly beef and tomatoes and corn, perk it up with chile con carne seasoning (not chili powder) and make it thick enough to serve on sliced leftover Double Duty Corn Bread. A gourmet "Sloppy Joe"!

Chapter 7

...*Baking Tips*...

Home baking is almost a lost art for millions of home-makers in our modern world. Commercial bakeries or the local supermarket's baked-goods department supply an enormous quantity (but not necessarily *quality*) of breads, pastries, and party snacks for no more effort or time than a short trip to the store. Some low sodium breads and cookies are now available, although many contain a sodium level that is still too high to be acceptable for the strict limits we recommend. Check ingredients on the label carefully before buying.

Home baking can be a satisfying hobby—creative, challenging, and rewarding. If you have not discovered this from a scheduled "baking day" in your present weekly program, this is a good time to do so. Jokes about store-bought bread made of "tenderized foam rubber," and "bleached cardboard pie crust," will begin to have more meaning for you! Oven-baked items in the bread-and-cakes category are sure to be much better tasting when they come fresh from your own oven, served hot or still warm. *And* you know the ingredients are wholesome for the entire family.

While you are still a novice at this kind of creative endeavor, here are a few basic rules to keep in mind:

Follow the recipe exactly. This means precise amounts of ingredients, using measuring cups and measuring spoons—not tea cups and table silver; otherwise the amounts will not add up to the required quantity. A young neighbor discovered that the hard way. The recipe called for two cups of dried cranberries. Her measuring cup held 8 ounces and the box the berries came in noted its contents at 16 ounces. She used the whole box, unaware that *its* label referred to weight, not volume, and that the contents were equivalent to four times the two cups indicated in the recipe! Moral: No matter what weight or volume is listed on a package, follow the *recipe's* directions for measurements.

Every cook should have a set of measuring spoons (*not* scoops), and two measuring cups: a one-cup size and a two-cup size. Having both is a time-saving convenience when a recipe calls for dry and liquid ingredients to be measured separately.

Timing and temperatures may be varied depending upon the individual oven and, in some instances, damp weather. To adjust to these factors always check a new recipe in your oven *before* the directions indicate the cooking time is up. Eventually it will be sufficient to look, sniff, and touch, no matter when the handy automatic timer's bell rings.

The following five treats selected from the recipe section will give you an easy, rewarding start and please the whole family:

> Freckled Banana Bread
> One-Bowl Oatmeal Cookies
> Fern Lodge Muffins
> Florence's Butterscotch Brownies
> Kay's No-Cheating Chocolate Cake

Having discovered the joys and economy of low sodium baking, move on to more creative recipes for special occasions or everyday good feasting. See Chapter 4 for items and sources of supply for low sodium ingredients used in the suggested recipes.

Things to Remember

When measuring flour, scoop it lightly into the measuring cup. Do not pack it down or bounce the cup to make it settle.

When pouring batter into a pan add an extra table-spoonful to each corner. This tends to produce a more even cake with no hump in the middle. An uneven surface can also result if the oven is too hot or more flour than necessary has been used.

Let the cake cool in its pan on a cake rack for five minutes after removing it from the oven. This allows air to circulate evenly around it. Then loosen the sides of the cake with a spatula and shift it onto the rack for longer cooling.

When frosting a thoroughly cooled cake, pile the frosting on the top rather than doing the sides first. This way you can ease the frosting down the sides and avoid picking up crumbs.

While packaged pre-sifted flour produces entirely acceptable results, resifting will achieve a finer texture. To save time and work use a double or triple sifter—a gadget that does the job in one operation. If you don't have a sifter, get the multiple one with two or three sieves.

When using yeast in a recipe check the package to be sure the date for usability has not expired. Also, remember that too much heat ruins yeast's action. To dissolve it use lukewarm, not hot, liquid.

Ice water and thoroughly chilled shortening are vital to a successful pie crust. For superb flavor in a fruit pie's crust use half ice water and half cold fruit juice. During a hot spell the best results will be obtained by mixing pastry dough quickly in a pre-chilled bowl with cold utensils.

If pastry dough cracks while rolling it out, ice water used sparingly will "glue" it together. Ice water will help to join top and bottom crusts, make filled-in patches adhere properly.

Unlike pastry, which should be mixed rapidly, yeast dough must never be hurried. It should be covered lightly with a clean soft cloth, such as a tea towel, and allowed to rise slowly in a warm—not hot—place away from drafts. Do *not* put it in the oven or on a radiator to hurry the rising.

To prevent a dry, cracked crust from forming on rising dough, spread a little corn oil over the surface before covering.

Speedy mixing together of dry and liquid ingredients makes lighter muffins. Do *not* beat the batter. Stir only until all flour is evenly moistened. But *popover* batter should be beaten to the consistency of heavy cream.

Learn to understand the idiosyncracies of your baking oven. Normally recipes properly prepared will turn out the same whether baked in an electric or gas oven, or in a wood-burning camp range, although this last is likely to be much hotter and consequently take less time. Do your own experimenting with temperature and timing. Overcooked baking is a disaster; undercooking can always be rectified if more time is required for any reason.

———————

Keep in mind that having several things in the oven at the same time may affect the baking time, although it will not interfere with the success of a recipe if it has been correctly prepared at the start. One exception is important to note: *popovers require an oven all to themselves!* Anything else baking in the same oven at the same time may affect the temperature just enough to deflate those delicately rising popovers.

Chapter 8

... Adapting Your Own
Recipes ...

Undoubtedly you have your own favorite recipes. These need not be abandoned unless they require ingredients that are naturally high in sodium. Many recipes can be adapted successfully as you gain experience in preparing low sodium dishes, but it is advisable to discard an individual recipe if there is considerable doubt as to its suitability.

Numerous alternatives for the usual ingredients in standard recipes are listed in Chapter 4. Low sodium fruits and vegetables are listed alphabetically on page 103. The following summary provides practical general guidance for revising your favorite recipes or those found in other cookbooks:

ASPICS, MOLDS	Use plain unflavored gelatin with any pure juices, meat or fish stock, or low sodium bouillon cubes. In place of salt use vinegar, juice of lime or lemon. For salad molds use Aunt Emma's Boil-Up Dressing (page 106) instead of regular mayonnaise.

BAKING
POWDER

Use the low sodium formula given on page 10, which can be made up at your drugstore, but use one-half *more* of this than a non-adapted recipe calls for. (Example: for 1 teaspoon regular baking powder use 1½ teaspoons of low sodium formula.)

BAKING SODA
(Sodium
Bicarbonate)

Substitute *potassium* bicarbonate, available at drugstores, and use the same amount as of regular baking soda.

CANNING,
PRESERVING

The amount of salt called for in such recipes is not sufficient to be an actual preservative. Therefore omit it and proceed with directions. Vinegar or ascorbic acid, if indicated, is acceptable.

COOLERS,
PUNCHES

Do not use commercial soft drinks or tonics in these. Combine water or club soda (wine if permitted) with citrus fruit juices, apricot nectar, apple cider. A dash of fresh lemon juice revitalizes approved canned juices. Perk them up with flavorings: peppermint extract, clove, cinnamon, allspice.

CHOCOLATE

Substitute Hershey brand cocoa.

CREAM

Use regular cream. Avoid non-dairy creamers or aerosol whipped toppings.

FLOUR	Use any except self-rising or dark rye.
FRUIT	Sun-dried, fresh. Check labels on canned or frozen fruit for salt or sodium preservatives.
HERBS, SPICES	Most of these are satisfactory. See complete list of approved ones on page 30.
LARD	Never permissible. Use vegetable shortening.
MILK	If skim milk is allowed by physician, use it. Otherwise, follow label directions for reconstituting low sodium milk powder. (See Chapter 4 for brand names.)
NUTS	Use only unsalted nuts. Available whole or chopped in health food stores, large supermarkets.
OIL	Use polyunsaturated types such as corn or safflower oil.
SALT	No recipe really needs it. Substitute lemon juice.
SAUCES, GRAVIES	Use low sodium milk or regular cream, your own meat stock, or low sodium bouillon cubes. Low sodium cream soups make good sauce bases.

SHERBET　　　Follow any recipe for these or ices, using water or low sodium milk. Can be made in ice cube tray.

SHORTENING　Use salt-free corn oil margarine. If doctor permits, salt-free sweet butter is available in supermarkets.

SUGAR　　　　Any variety except *dark* brown. Light brown sugar may be used in any recipe calling for dark.

The ingredients in most baked goods are easily adapted to low sodium recipes. Once your own collection of recipes has been converted to this special cookery, you will find many new ideas in family magazines and daily newspapers. These can be adapted and added to your collection, giving you an unlimited variety of wholesome, exciting dishes for every occasion.

Chapter 9

...Freezer Freedom...

Whether your freezer is part of the refrigerator or a separate unit, every square inch of it will save time and food money. You can have harvest-fresh fruit and vegetables year round at a substantial saving if you buy at the peak of the growing season when prices are lowest. This also applies to meat, fish, and poultry. Stock up when such items are on sale or in seasonal supply when prices are reduced. Clean, cut, and prepare as may be necessary; wrap and freeze in family-size portions, making sure each package is dated. Most fruits and vegetables will keep from 8 to 12 months; home-baked low sodium pies, cakes, and cookies, 2 to 10 months; meat (depending on variety and cut) from 3 to 12 months; and fish will maintain good quality in the freezer up to 9 months. All, of course, must be stored at 0 degrees Farenheit or lower.

A number of air-tight protective wrappings may be used: plastic freezer bags, laminated freezer paper, heavy-duty aluminum foil, plastic or metal containers. All are available at supermarkets and hardware stores. Or, reuse coffee cans, plastic margarine tubs, and other suitable tight-closing containers. When baking bread-stuffs for freezing and subsequent reheating as needed, double the recipe and use aluminum foil muffin tins or loaf pans. These come in various sizes and are space savers in the freezer because they can be stacked, wrapped in foil or heavy plastic bags.

Actual freezing procedures are simple. Most vegetables need only to be prepared for cooking and placed in plain boiling water for two to ten minutes (depending on the texture of the vegetable), then drained, cooled, and placed in the freezer. For example, chopped onions require 2 minutes of cooking, corn on the cob, 8 minutes. Fruit may be packed in sugar syrup, dry sugar, or left unsweetened. Fish is highly perishable and must be fresh, thoroughly cleaned, and frozen the day it is bought or caught. It is not necessary to dip it in any preserving solution, although most booklets on freezing recommend it. In any event, do *not* use salt.

Most manufacturers of refrigerator-freezers or individual freezers include such directions in pamphlets which come with the appliances. If you require or wish further information, the following government publications are inexpensive and dependable:

Freezing Meat and Fish in the Home. Home and Garden Bulletin No. 93, U.S. Department of Agriculture. Price 25 cents. 23 pages.

Home Freezing of Fruits and Vegetables. Home and Garden Bulletin No. 10, U.S. Department of Agriculture. Price 20 cents. 47 pages.

Before ordering these it might be well to check with the government center near you. If not available there send check or money order (no stamps or cash) to: Superintendent of Documents, U.S. Government Printing Office, Washington, D.C. 20402.

Since a majority of the recipes presented here can be frozen and stored, you will find it convenient to increase quantities of ingredients indicated in those recipes most frequently served so that you will be cooking for the freezer as well as the family in a single session. This method also will save gas and electricity.

The following tips will enable you to take the fullest advantage of your freezer's daily service:

Freeze stock made from meat or fish bones in ice cube trays. When solid, pop the cubes out and store in a heavy plastic bag. Remove any quantity from the freezer as need for sauces, soups, and casserole liquid.

✸

Puree leftover vegetables or fruit in the blender. Use same ice cube procedure as above. These cubes make instant pure baby food in small easy-to-heat portions. Excellent in gelatin desserts or molded salads, too.

✸

Make casseroles, hash, stews, etc., as usual but in quantity. Cool, then freeze in meal-sized portions.

✸

Store the crusts and ends from stale low sodium bread in a plastic bag until you accumulate enough to make poultry stuffing or bread crumbs. For the latter, put defrosted bread pieces in the blender long enough to reduce them to crumbs. Store in freezer in screw-top plastic or glass jar.

✸

Prepare non-lettuce sandwiches for school or office, tea party, or other entertaining ahead of time. Freeze flat, well wrapped. If for lunch, they will defrost in time if you take them out at breakfast. Use low sodium bread. Do not attempt to freeze cracker canapes of any kind.

Go easy on your budget by saving even the smallest amounts of leftovers. Store scraps of assorted cooked vegetables, diced meat, and flaked fish in separate and labeled freezer jars or bags, adding any bits as they accumulate. Such mixed vegetables can be heated up for a "spring medley," can be used in salads, or can be combined with the diced meat or fish to make mixtures for stuffed green peppers, meat pies, noodle or rice casseroles. Also use them to enrich low sodium canned soups.

*

Chop fresh chives, parsley, green pepper, or herbs and store them in separate plastic sandwich bags. Place these bags in a larger heavy one with a twist-tie for extra protection. These defrost quickly and have a more delicate flavor than commercial dried herbs.

*

When preparing fresh oranges, limes, or lemons, do not discard the rinds. Store in a plastic bag in the freezer. Slivered peels add a special continental seasoning to meat and fish dishes. Lemon peel for fish, chicken, and veal; orange peel for beef stew, duck, and pork. Frozen rind is also much easier to grate for cakes, puddings, or dessert sauces.

*

Leftover thin pancakes (see recipe, page 114) may be spread with preserves or pure jelly, rolled up, and frozen; reheat in a slow oven and sprinkle with powdered sugar for a spectacular dessert. Or spread with a meat filling, roll up, and serve with sauce made with low sodium cream of mushroom soup.

*

Avoid the monotony of leftovers. Freeze slices of roast, meat loaf, or poultry. Reheat for serving as needed in foil in the oven, or in a skillet with sauce made from frozen meat-stock cubes, and any additions such as onions, mushrooms, etc.

❋

To keep fresh fruits such as strawberries, peaches, or apricots from darkening, dip them in a solution made from dissolved ascorbic acid crystals (available at most drugstores). Proper proportions are given in the government bulletin on freezing fruits and vegetables. Do not freeze fruit or tomatoes in foil wrap.

❋

Foods tend to expand as they freeze. When filling containers be sure to leave at least an inch of space at the top.

❋

Government bulletins on freezing fish recommend only salt for pre-freezing treatment. The use of salt is not necessary. But if you want to improve the quality of stored big fish or thick fish steaks, dip them in a solution of ascorbic acid crystals (available at drugstores) made from 1 tablespoon of crystals to ½ gallon of water.

❋

Thaw all frozen foods in their freezer wrappings.

❋

Some foods do not respond well to freezing. Among these are:

Egg white frostings	Meringue	Sour cream
Eggs in shells	Custard	Whipped cream
Hard-cooked eggs	Fried foods	Potato salad
Fresh tomatoes	Raw potatoes	Unblanched
Raw apples	Cucumber	vegetables
		Lettuce

Chapter 10

... *On the Town* ...

There is no reason to conclude that your specially stocked kitchen provides the only available "oasis" for proper meals. Eating out—at other people's homes or in restaurants—can be made completely enjoyable occasions by a little simple planning on your part. You do not need to forgo picnics, backyard get-togethers, or beach and tailgate parties; nor, as you will learn from the next chapter, do you need to cancel plans for vacations, cruises, or a stay at a resort hotel. A low sodium regime is adaptable to almost any social or festive occasion since it provides a wide variety of foods from which to choose.

The key words are "planning" and "selection." Choice makes the difference. And choice is yours. Making that choice need not be handled dramatically or ostentatiously, because many foods served in private homes or in public eating places are acceptable to a low sodium program without adaptation. However there are dishes which may not adhere to the low sodium standard because of high natural sodium or certain inadvisable ingredients used in preparation.

On the following pages are suggestions that have worked best for us.

Workaday Lunches

Sandwiches made at home and kept fresh in insulated bags are an ideal answer to proper lunches, but of course not the only one. Using a variety of fillings will help dispel monotony from sandwich lunches, as will extra treats made from the cookie recipes in this book.

If you normally prepare a hearty breakfast for your family, a take-along lunch is usually sufficient at midday. Nor do you need to look as though you had missed the school bus! A man-size lunch will fit into an attaché case without crowding briefs, charts, or other papers. Women's handbags are usually fairly roomy; or you can utilize one of the decorative tote-bags which are popular today.

Office buildings have corridor or lobby hot-drink machines or coffee shops; many companies have their own cafeterias. Some business-district lunch counters provide take-out or telephone order service. Any of these is a source for coffee, tea, or fruit juice to accompany your take-along lunch.

All sandwiches should be made with low sodium bread. What you put in them depends on whatever is on hand at home. Try thin-sliced roast beef with a sprinkling of Bakon Yeast; low sodium water-pack tuna or salmon, flaked and mixed with Aunt Emma's Boil-Up Dressing (recipe on page 106). Or use cold chicken or turkey white meat with cranberry sauce as a spread instead of the usual salt-free margarine. Low sodium peanut butter with pure jelly is always an easy favorite. Sliced cold meat loaf or pot roast spread with low sodium chili sauce makes a hunger-appeasing sandwich treat.

If you choose to make your own low sodium bread, the recipe for Mother's English Tea Loaf (page 71) is

sure to be to your liking. Or you will find several
commercial-brand low sodium breads in supermarket
freezer sections and some health food stores. Your local
bakery is another possible source, as suggested on
page 18. Wherever you purchase it, keep in mind that
a salt-free bread is not necessarily a low sodium loaf,
and may not be acceptable to your eating program
unless it is water-based or made with low sodium milk
powder.

A time-saving trick which will keep sandwiches
fresh is to make them in advance and freeze them flat,
well wrapped. Do *not* freeze any sandwiches whose
fillings are prepared with low sodium mayonnaise, lettuce, or egg whites. However, you can safely use these
ingredients in foods that are prepared ahead of time
for use the same day, keeping them refrigerated but
not frozen.

If you do not take lunch to work there is still no
reason to starve. Most people in offices or other busi-
ness pursuits tend to frequent one or two favorite
restaurants or lunch counters. Often the service is
better when waitresses and counter-servers know you
as a steady customer. When you consider the competi-
tion among restaurants it is understandable that an
establishment which can count on your daily patronage
will be quite happy to cater to your special needs. Ask
them to store small quantities of low sodium foods for
you which you will bring in periodically: low sodium
crackers and canned soups, for example, to go along
with acceptable items on the regular menu.

If this proves to be too much trouble, most eating
places catering to noontime customers are sure to have
several items on the daily menu which fit your requirements without special preparation. Use honest
judgment in your selections; and when you do "go
overboard" for some reason, offset any possible ill

effects by being particularly selective during the next two or three days. When lunching with friends or customers, simplify your order.

Restaurant Dining

Few men will object to skipping the cooked vegetables. And in most restaurants they *should* be skipped if you are on a low sodium program, for such large eating places routinely use salt in the cooking water for all vegetables. Some even add a touch of baking soda (a sodium) to maintain the fresh color in green vegetables. But you are not likely to feel deprived considering the wide selection of other foods available to you.

For the main course select a slice of any roast—veal, beef, lamb, poultry, or fresh pork (but not ham) may be ordered without gravy. Simplify this by requesting an "inside cut." The surface of any roast is sure to have been generously seasoned before cooking. For the same reason, trim away the edges of the slice. Instead of gravy that is undoubtedly salted in preparation, order an accompaniment such as applesauce, mint jelly, or cranberry sauce.

If you choose chicken or turkey be sure to specify white meat. Dark meat, as well as the skin, is higher in sodium. You may also order any chop or steak to be broiled without salt or other seasoning at your request. Fresh fish (but not shellfish) cooked the same way and served with half a lemon makes an excellent main course. Be sure the fish *is* fresh, not frozen. Frozen fish is usually subjected to a salt bath or brine in processing. If there is any possibility that the fish being served is not fresh it is best to order another main course.

Along with meat or fish main dishes, have a baked potato topped with sour cream, or seasoned with pepper and paprika. Add to this a fresh salad with plain oil and vinegar dressing. Avoid mayonnaise or dressings made with various cheeses.

Cocktails are permissible if your doctor has approved them for you. Some on a low sodium regime may not have that approval for other reasons. Whether by preference or necessity, you may start a meal with apple cider, apricot nectar, or cranberry juice. For dessert: water-based sherbet or baked apple or a fruit pie *if* you avoid the crust.

When dining at a Chinese restaurant where selections are cooked to order there is no problem. Simply specify that the food be cooked without salt or MSG (monosodium glutamate), which is a favorite flavoring with oriental cooks. Obviously you must avoid soy sauce. Pepper, lemon juice, and sugar will enhance the flavors just as well and give them a distinctive sweet-sour fillip.

Accept with Pleasure

Dining at the homes of friends and relatives is a traditionally pleasant social occasion. Your low sodium regime need not interfere with these gatherings nor is it necessary for you to take your own food. Such a gesture would be an insult to your hostess, however graciously it might seem to be accepted, and embarrassing to you if your plate is conspicuously different from the others.

Tempting foods not permitted on your menu are quite easily bypassed if you treat yourself to an appetite-appeasing snack before going to the dinner where you expect such foods may be served. This lets you take small portions from the party table with no excessive strain on your will power. Since you have no way of knowing how any of the food was prepared— and for heaven's sake don't *ask!*—it is well to assume that the sodium count is higher than your daily limit. An occasional compromise with your restricted regime can safely be tolerated provided you make up for it by being very cautious for the next three or four days —the time usually required to rid the body of the extra sodium.

Buffet serving is the perfect solution to the low sodium diner's problem. You have more control over what goes onto your plate. Selections should be sensible and restraint exercised as to amounts. Small indulgences can be offset as suggested earlier. Home parties for which you have prepared the food or supervised the cooking pose no problem at all. Foods prepared with "adapted" recipes are sure to please everyone, with no one noticing anything special about the fare except its more delicious flavors. As with regular home meals, place salt containers on the table for those who may wish to use it on their nonrestricted food.

Official banquets, club affairs, and other such occasions may pose some problems, but none that cannot be handled—and certainly not enough to cause you to forgo the event. If it is an invitation affair for members and their guests, a copy of the menu frequently accompanies the invitation or is posted on the organization's bulletin board. In this case you can plan in advance the extent of your indulgence and determine how much of a snack to eat before going to the banquet. If it is a dues-paying affair you have no problem. You need only to arrange your choice with the manager ahead of time.

Fortunately modern entertaining is rather informal. Get-togethers are often impromptu, with each member of a group asked to bring an item or two as in the old custom of "covered dish suppers." If, as so often happens in New England, the occasion is a simple and sociable "dessert and coffee" held after your own family dinner at home, your contribution is easy. A cake, pie, or dessert bread from any of the recipes given here will do nicely. And there is no necessity for labeling your contribution "diet food"; it simply isn't. What you are providing is good old-fashioned flavor with no imitation ingredients or additives.

Of course, family get-togethers present no problem, nor do those with close friends who are considered part of the family. In New England all contribute to the meal for any reunion; it is good fun and good feasting. The buffet table is crowded with a marvelous variety of dishes, yet no individual cook has had to spend wearisome hours in the kitchen. (I never have any need to "explain" the food I provide, whether it is a casserole of low sodium tuna with rice, low sodium canned peas and mushrooms, or a selection of my adapted recipes for cookies, banana bread, and spice cake. And rarely is any left over!)

If your circle of friends subscribes to the B.Y.O.B. (bring your own bottle) custom when entertaining, so much the better. Most carbonated beverages contain sodium; simply use ice water or fruit juice as a mixer. If your doctor permits wine you can mix a superb punch made with apple cider or cranberry juice and a California table wine. This can be put into any bottle and taken to a party. When you are the hostess place a wine punch in an elegant bowl on the serving table along with bottles of liquor and carbonated mixers. You are pretty sure to find that you are not the only one favoring the punch bowl.

Chapter 11

... On the Road ...

Over the past several years my husband and I have taken automobile trips varying in duration from a few hours to two weeks, covering nine different states. The longer journeys necessitated stopping for meals and frequently staying overnight at hotels, motor inns, or occasionally at one of those old-fashioned country taverns which serves meals "family style." We enjoy such outings to the fullest without any need to depart from our controlled food regime.

General preparations for one of these trips are the same as most people make except that we add a few items to the food supply we take along. A large insulated picnic box, available at most stores where camping equipment is sold, is the perfect solution for packing low sodium bread, salt-free margarine, and an initial supply of reconstituted low sodium milk. A screw-top pint jar holds enough liquid milk for one day's travel. Powdered low sodium milk and a measuring spoon are also taken along for future mixing since the milk may not be readily available in stores along the way. Only the *reconstituted* milk need be kept in the picnic box, beside a plastic bag filled with ice cubes.

Cookies made from any of the recipes given here are long-lasting in terms of remaining fresh; perhaps *not* so lasting if some member of the traveling party is very fond of cookies! It is best to make a large batch just to be on the safe side. They may be baked weeks in advance of the projected trip and frozen until you are ready to pack up. They will stay fresh for a week or more on the road if you pack them in an air-tight container (tin or heavy plastic) which has a sure-closing lid. Keep them handy for nibbling along the way or as a bedtime snack.

Neither of *us* is likely to undertake the kind of outing that demands backpacking supplies for days in remote wilderness areas, nor are most people on restricted food regimes. We find plenty of large supermarkets near main highways, many of which carry low sodium canned goods in their diet foods sections. If you are sight-seeing in a small town you have not visited before, inquire about health food stores. Such shops are pretty sure to have some low sodium specialties produced locally. Perhaps you will find a gastronomic surprise—an edible souvenir to take home with you.

For a quick hot pick-me-up when driving long distances in the winter, take along cans of low sodium soups. Almost any roadside eating place will be glad to open a can and heat the contents for you if you explain the reason. They are accustomed to such requests as warming baby bottles, or putting food through a blender for a customer's sensitive innards. For more substantial meals, use the suggestions given in the previous chapter on restaurant lunches and dinners.

Breakfast on the road is never a problem. Fruit juice is available at any restaurant, as is a choice of acceptable cereals: regular puffed rice, puffed wheat, or shredded wheat biscuits. Hot cereal is permissible if it is the old fashioned *non-instant* cream of wheat or oatmeal. But most restaurants prepare hot cereal in advance, and salt the cooking water; so unless the cook is willing to prepare a salt-free serving for you, you would be wise to forgo the hot cereal.

Ask the waitress to put some of your mixed low sodium milk into a small pitcher for easy pouring, or if the place is very busy just spoon the milk from your jar onto the cereal. Or, since even a 200-milligram restriction of sodium per day permits two ounces of cream, thin the cream normally served with an equal amount of water, making enough cream for both cereal and beverage if desired. Cocoa as prepared in most public eating places is not advisable. It is safer to avoid it while traveling unless you have the means to prepare your own from the Hershey brand cocoa as recommended. The Dutch-process variety is laden with sodium and, of course, would be made with regular milk.

If your cholesterol intake is not strictly limited, a soft-boiled egg with pepper is delicious. Or an egg scrambled with water, not milk, cooked in vegetable oil or the salt-free margarine from your picnic box's supply. (One medium-size egg has about 60 mg. of sodium and 65 of good potassium.) Ask the waitress to toast a slice or two of your own low sodium bread, and use any pure jam or jelly as a spread.

The so-called "fast service" eating places need not be avoided if you are on a throughway which has no other restaurant that might have a wider choice on its menu. In addition to the familiar well-advertised establishments which dot the roadways from coast to coast, some states run similar food places on their convenient toll highways.

Rather than turn off the expressway and take the extra time to locate a more suitable restaurant, order an "emergency meal" at one of the available establishments. Your best bet is a hamburger, cooked without seasoning and served on *half* a bun (like an open-face sandwich), with a slice of tomato or cucumber—no relish, catsup, or mustard. Season it with pepper and lemon juice, if available. With it, have your choice of fruit juice, coffee, or tea, and for dessert any fresh or canned fruit, or a fruit cup, but skip the maraschino cherry or non-dairy topping.

The sodium content of drinking water is naturally high in many areas of the country, although this is a matter of concern only for those whose daily sodium allowance is particularly strict. In such cases, it is best to use bottled water. This is now available under various brand names in supermarkets and many smaller food shops. The label on the bottle lists sodium content in milligrams. A half-gallon jug takes little space in an automobile and the supply can be replenished along the way.

But what about that dream vacation?

You need *not* cancel your reservation if you are on a restricted food regime. Airlines, cruise ships, and resort hotels are prepared to welcome you on your own terms. A little simple planning, and perhaps a little more self-control, will let you have that best-of-all vacation. But again, *you* must do the planning.

When making your reservation for a plane trip to the vacation spot, inquire as to the number of meals to be served during the flight and, if possible, what choices are on the menu. Order your portions cooked to your low sodium specifications. Most airlines advertise their eagerness to cater to any food requirements, and low sodium needs are commonplace as well as being simple to satisfy. Just be certain that what you want is clearly understood at the time you make your reservation *and* confirmed by phone well before you get on the plane. If such planning does go awry for some reason, make selections judiciously from the general menu—a plain baked potato and unseasoned steak, for example. If these are not available, a meal that may not adhere fully to your particular sodium restriction can be offset by extra care when again you can make your own choices.

With few exceptions, mealtime service on trains today is generally designed for the casual traveler. This varies from a snack bar to a fully equipped dining car, depending upon the railroad company and the length of the journey. If your trip is one that involves several hours, it is best to take along your own sandwiches and have them in the snack bar with coffee or tea. If you are going to be on the train overnight or longer, you should check with the railroad company or your travel agent ahead of time and make the special arrangements necessary for your meals.

The basic concept of any cruise ship is to pamper the passengers. There is no reason why that cannot apply to you. Here, especially, a gastronomic spree for all on board is anticipated from embarkation to landing, and is one of the main attractions when making the decision about the cruise you take.

You need not feel cheated because of your special food regime.

The head chef is responsible for all menus, of course, and most dishes are prepared by a number of assistants with professional skills in a variety of foods. You may be surprised to learn that a *whole list* of restricted food plans are prepared for every meal on such cruises or transoceanic voyages. Meals are arranged for diabetics, allergies, ulcers, low cholesterol, low roughage, carbohydrate-free, high protein food programs, and meals for travelers with low blood sugar problems, along with several other more complicated mealtime restrictions.

Most vacationers arrange for cruises and ocean trips through travel agencies. All you need do is provide the agency with a list of items needed for preparing your special foods: low sodium bread and milk, salt-free margarine (or, if permitted, unsalted sweet butter which is usually the choice of gourmet chefs), and any other items you feel are important to your meals; give instructions that vegetables be cooked without salt, meat and poultry without seasoning, and that no sauces or gravies be served with your portions. The chef will take care of all this for you. You will probably have your meals served at the same table each day, making it easy for your waiter to take care of your servings discreetly.

These guidelines also apply to the stateroom steward should you wish a picnic basket prepared to take ashore on a sight-seeing trip, or a late-night snack in your cabin. Request that bottled water be made available at your table and in your stateroom if the water used on the ship is of high sodium content. The ship's doctor probably has this information. It is quite likely that bottled water (spring or distilled) is routinely carried on such cruises since many special food regimes dictate it.

Resort hotel service is no less regal, or lacking in special attentions.

The best way to avoid misunderstanding about food needs is to write to the hotel in advance, outlining the reason for your food regime and the items necessary to maintain it. Ask for a written reply and inquire about any extra charge that may be made for providing special cookery. None of this preparation should be complicated considering the many special diets adhered to for various reasons. But occasionally a hotel will make an extra charge for such a service and you may want to know about it before confirming your reservation.

Thus, with a minimum of sensible planning you are reasonably assured of maximum enjoyment on your vacation regardless of the mode of travel or your destination.

RECIPES

Breads and Muffins

DAVID'S DATE-NUT BREAD

8 oz. pitted sun-dried dates
1 teaspoon potassium bicarbonate*
1 cup hot water
1 cup granulated sugar
2 egg yolks, room temperature
1¾ cups pastry flour
1½ teaspoons vanilla
½ cup chopped unsalted nuts
2 egg whites, room temperature

Preheat oven 350°.
Cut dates in small pieces into mixing bowl. Sprinkle potassium bicarbonate over them. Add hot water. Blend, let stand until cool. Add sugar, beaten egg yolks, flour, vanilla, and nuts. Beat egg whites until stiff, fold into dough mixture. Pour into 5″ x 9″ nonstick loaf pan. Bake 50 minutes. Turn oven to 325°, bake 10 minutes more or until cake tester comes out dry. Cool on cake rack.

---

*Remember this about potassium bicarbonate: If it hardens into a seemingly solid block (a commonplace condition which does not affect its quality), simply spoon-scrape the amount needed for a recipe.

GLAZED ORANGE BREAD

2 medium oranges
½ cup sun-dried raisins
½ cup chopped unsalted walnuts
½ cup salt-free margarine, room temperature
1 cup granulated sugar
2 eggs, room temperature
2 cups all-purpose flour
1 teaspoon potassium bicarbonate

Preheat oven 350°.
Squeeze juice from oranges, set aside for glaze. Grind seeded orange rinds with food chopper (not a blender) along with raisins and nuts. In separate bowl, cream margarine, sugar, add unbeaten eggs singly, mixing well after each addition. Blend flour and potassium bicarbonate together, add to creamed mixture alternately with the fruit-nut ingredients—about ⅓ each at a time, blending. Turn into non-stick 5″ x 9″ loaf pan lined the long way with sprayed foil extending over ends. Bread removes easily. Bake 1 hour in center of oven. If cake tester comes out sticky bake another 10-15 minutes. When done, top with:

SPOON GLAZE

Cook reserved orange juice with ½ cup granulated sugar in saucepan until slightly thickened. Pour over warm baked bread. Cool. Wrap in foil and refrigerate until next day, or freeze. Aging enhances the flavor.

DOUBLE-DUTY CORN BREAD

This quick marvel is a splendid addition to luncheon or supper casseroles, a special breakfast treat, or mid-morning coffee break. Make plenty of it! Serve fresh from the oven, or slice cold ½ inch thick, spread with salt-free margarine, sprinkle with cinnamon sugar, and toast under broiler flame, checking flame for correct timing.

Preheat oven 350°.
In a large mixing bowl, blend thoroughly:

1¾ cups all-purpose flour
⅔ cup granulated sugar
⅓ cup corn meal—white or yellow
3 teaspoons low sodium baking powder

In a separate bowl, beat together:

1 cup Featherweight liquid milk
¼ cup corn oil
2 eggs, room temperature

Add second mixture to first and blend the two together. Pour or spoon contents of bowl into 8″ square non-stick pan. Bake about 35 minutes. Better test at 30 minutes. *Makes* 9 squares—18 when split, or 8 slices—16 split.

Variations: Add about ¼ cup diced green pepper and/or a handful of chopped nuts or 2 teaspoons minced parsley while blending ingredients. Check the ingredients under Salad Fruits, Vegetables & Greens (page

103) for other ideas to make recipe more colorful and piquant. Just be sure not to add anything mushy which will cause the bread to lose texture.

Southern Accent: Old-fashioned iron cornstick pans are now available. Recipe makes 21 corn sticks, baked 25 minutes at 425°. Can be frozen for later use. They freeze perfectly and are great re-heated for breakfast.

CLAIRE'S LEMON DESSERT BREAD

1 cup granulated sugar
½ cup vegetable shortening
2 eggs, room temperature
1½ cups all-purpose flour
1½ teaspoons low sodium baking powder
½ cup Featherweight liquid milk
grated rind of 2 lemons
1 teaspoon lemon extract

Preheat oven 350°.
Cream shortening, sugar, grated rind, and lemon extract. Add eggs singly, unbeaten. Beat well. Blend flour and baking powder. Add alternately with milk, about ⅛ each, to mixture, stirring vigorously. Pour into 5″ x 9″ non-stick loaf pan, or line with foil. Bake about 55 minutes or until cake tester comes out dry.

GLAZE

Add juice of 1 lemon to ½ cup granulated sugar, stir until dissolved. Dribble over top of cake bread when removed from oven. Cool at least 5 hours before cutting. Keeps well in refrigerator; also may be frozen in foil-wrap.

Hint: If you line the loaf pan the long way with sprayed foil that extends over the ends, bread will be easy to remove to cake rack to cool.

MOTHER'S ENGLISH TEA LOAF

(This recipe, handed down from my English grandmother, originally called for salt. Adapted to new ingredients, its flavor is enhanced rather than diminished.)

Into a large warm bowl put:

> 1½ cups warm tap water
> 1 package dry yeast, sprinkled on the water
> 2 tablespoons granulated sugar
> 2 tablespoons corn oil

Let stand for 5 minutes then beat thoroughly with heavy fork. Add 4 rounded cups all-purpose flour, *one* cup at a time, beating until dough is blended. Put dough in oiled bowl, turn dough over to oil the top. Cover with a light towel and put in a warm place until it rises to double its original bulk (takes about 1 hour). Turn out on floured board, cut in half, shape into loaves, put in greased glass loaf pans. Let the loaves rise, covered, to top of pans (about 45 minutes).

Preheat oven about 15 minutes before baking loaves at 350° for 30 minutes. Turn out on rack to cool.

Variation: My grandmother preferred this dough made into typical English tea cakes (for, obviously, typical English tea-time) and they're great for American brunch. Add raisins to the mixture, divide into 6 individual cakes instead of 2 loaves. Arrange in a large greased roasting pan for the second 45-50 minutes rise. Bake as above. Serve hot. Slice and toast if any are left over.

FRECKLED BANANA BREAD

3 very ripe bananas—4 if small
1 cup granulated sugar
1 egg, room temperature
¼ cup corn oil
1½ cups all-purpose flour, mixed with
1 teaspoon potassium bicarbonate

Preheat oven 325°.
Put peeled, cut bananas in mixing bowl and mash thoroughly with fork. Add all other ingredients and blend together. Pour into non-stick 5″ x 9″ loaf pan. Bake 1 hour. Cool on cake rack before cutting. Keeps days in refrigerator; freezes well, too.

Variation: Add ½ cup chopped unsalted walnuts before baking. See Appendix for dietary counts on both versions.

FERN LODGE MUFFINS

¼ cup salt-free melted margarine or corn oil
⅓ cup granulated sugar
1 egg, room temperature
1 cup Featherweight liquid milk

2 cups all-purpose or super-fine flour
4 teaspoons low sodium baking powder

Preheat oven 400°.
Cream sugar with margarine or oil. Add egg and continue beating. Add milk gradually. Blend flour and baking powder, add to bowl. Mix thoroughly. Bake in non-stick Pam-sprayed muffin tins 15 minutes.

Variations:
1. Sprinkle tops with cinnamon-sugar mix before baking.
2. Add 1 cup fresh drained blueberries to batter.
3. Rub dot-sized sugar cubes over orange or lemon skin to extract the oil, then dip into fresh fruit juice and insert into center of each uncooked muffin. This provides both glaze and unique flavor.
4. Add ¼ cup wheat germ to batter for added taste and texture.
5. Use the muffins, split, for old-fashioned fruit or berry shortcake.
6. Try your own variations—split, spread, and broil to reheat if you wish.

This recipe freezes well. Warm in a slow oven a few minutes before serving.

POPOVERS ARE PUSHOVERS

Take six 5½-ounce custard cups and grease thoroughly with vegetable shortening.

Preheat oven to 425°.
In a medium-sized bowl put:

        2 eggs, room temperature
        1 cup Featherweight liquid milk

Blend with a fork. Add 1 cup all-purpose flour all at
once. Blend—do not overbeat. Fill custard cups ¾
full. Put on a cookie sheet for easy handling. Bake 40-
45 minutes in center of oven. Do not open oven door;
constant heat is vital. When done, loosen with spatula,
serve promptly.

Hint: If you're serving more people, this recipe will
make 8 or 9 smaller popovers, depending on size of
custard cups. They won't look as dramatic or pop as
high but will be equally welcome. Try both ways and
decide for yourself.

Note: While all-purpose flour makes perfectly acceptable popovers, I prefer to use the super-fine variety,
which produces lighter, puffier ones.

APRIL FOOL'S GINGERBREAD

This looks and tastes like old-fashioned gingerbread—
but with not a drop of molasses!

        ½ cup salt-free margarine, softened
        1 cup granulated sugar
        1 egg, room temperature
        1 cup applesauce (see recipe, page 111)
        1¾ cups all-purpose flour
        1 teaspoon potassium bicarbonate
        2 teaspoons commercial apple pie spice
        dash of ground cloves

Preheat oven 350°.

Cream margarine and sugar. Add egg and beat until fluffy. In separate bowl, blend flour, potassium bicarbonate, and spices. Beat applesauce into first mixture, then blend flour-spice mix into it. Spoon batter into greased 8″ x 8″ pan. Bake 40 minutes. Turn off heat, leave in oven another 12 minutes. Turn out on rack to cool. Cut into squares or slices. Serve topped with whipped margarine or snowy frosting (see recipes, pages 114 and 78). Or try warm applesauce on it.

Cupcakes: Spoon batter into greased muffin tins and bake in preheated 350° oven for 18 minutes. Fill tins about ¾ full. Makes 18 cupcakes. Frost with water-thinned marshmallow topping or your favorite cake topping.

Variations: Add ½ cup chopped unsalted nuts or ½ cup sun-dried raisins to the batter before baking, or use both, half-and-half.

Cakes

———— ❈ ————

FATHER'S FAVORITE SPONGE CAKE

Father was so fond of this cake that I learned to vary the basic recipe to make several different kinds of cakes. An 8″ x 8″ square pan makes a fine size for a variety of shortcakes: strawberry, peach—any fruit in season. It's great simply dusted with confectioner's sugar and served with morning coffee, afternoon tea, or after dinner. Change the pan, change the name—a 9″ round one makes it Boston Cream Pie, with a custard filling added. A 5″ x 10″ jelly-roll pan? Bake, spread with your pet filling, roll it up. Take off from there with your own ideas!

2 eggs, room temperature
1 cup vanilla sugar (see recipe, page 115)
1 cup cake flour
2 teaspoons low sodium baking powder
½ cup hot Featherweight liquid milk
1 generous teaspoon vanilla extract
½ teaspoon lemon extract

Preheat oven 350°.
Beat flavorings and eggs 2 minutes. Continue beating while adding vanilla sugar. Blend flour and baking powder, then alternating in smallish amounts, add this and hot milk as you mix all ingredients. Bake in what-

ever pan you choose for about 30 minutes (less for jelly roll), or when cake tester comes out dry. Refrigerates and freezes well.

AUNT JEANIE'S APPLESAUCE CAKE

1 cup granulated sugar
½ cup salt-free margarine
¼ teaspoon cinnamon
1 cup sun-dried raisins
1 teaspoon potassium bicarbonate
1 cup applesauce—canned or homemade
1¾ cups all-purpose flour

Preheat oven 350°.
Cream sugar with margarine. Blend in cinnamon and raisins. Separately, dissolve potassium bicarbonate in a bit of warm water, add to other ingredients. Fold in applesauce. Gradually mix in flour. Turn blend into sprayed non-stick 5″ x 9″ loaf pan. Sprinkle top with vanilla sugar (see recipe, page 115), and bake 1 hour. Check with cake tester. Bake another 10-15 minutes if needed. Cut when cooled on cake rack.

Whether the applesauce is plain or sweetened is up to you and your family's preference. I prefer my own spice-happy applesauce instead of canned, but either way is very tasty. Cake keeps moistly fresh in refrigerator.

Hint: This cake is particularly welcome in summer. Prepare and freeze while the weather is still cool enough so that you can stand an hour of oven heat. Bake several, cool, foil-wrap, and date the packages.

Then you are all set for those sizzling hate-the-kitchen days. Not that it isn't good year round!

KAY'S NO-CHEATING CHOCOLATE CAKE WITH SNOWY FROSTING

Into an 8″ x 8″ square ungreased pan sift:

> 1½ cups all-purpose flour
> 1 cup granulated sugar
> 3 tablespoons Hershey's cocoa
> 1 teaspoon potassium bicarbonate

Add:

> 6 tablespoons corn oil
> 1 tablespoon cider vinegar
> 1½ teaspoons vanilla extract
> 1 cup cold water

Preheat oven 350°.

Blend all ingredients very thoroughly, being attentive to the corners (a fork works fine for this). It will take a few minutes to insure full blending. Bake 35-40 minutes, checking with cake tester.

While this is in the oven, prepare:

SNOWY FROSTING

1 unbeaten egg white, room temperature
¾ cup granulated sugar (fine grain if you have it)
¼ teaspoon cream of tartar
2 tablespoons cold water

Place in top of double boiler and cook over boiling water, beating constantly for 7-8 minutes. For this, use a wire whisk, electric or hand beater. Remove from heat and continue to beat until it holds firm, perky peaks. Transfer cooled cake from rack to platter, spread frosting in whitecap fashion on top and sides. Decorate with sprinkles of chocolate "Jimmies."

ALMA'S SOUR CREAM SPICE CAKE

½ cup salt-free margarine, room temperature
1 cup *light* brown sugar, firmly packed
½ cup granulated sugar
2 cups (scant) all-purpose flour
3 teaspoons low sodium baking powder
½ teaspoon potassium bicarbonate
½ teaspoon nutmeg
1 teaspoon (generous) cinnamon
2 eggs, room temperature
1 cup commercial sour cream
1 teaspoon vanilla extract (optional)

Preheat oven 350°.
Cream margarine and both sugars together. Add eggs singly, beating all thoroughly. Separately, make a blend of flour, baking powder, potassium bicarbonate, nutmeg, cinnamon. Add this mix to first one gradually (⅛ at a time), beating after each addition. Mixture will be stiff. Add sour cream (and vanilla, if you want it) last and fork all to a smooth consistency. Pour into a sprayed 9″ tube pan. Bake 40-45 minutes or until cake tester comes out dry. Turn out carefully on cake rack to cool. Refrigerate or freeze.

Variation: ½ cup chopped unsalted walnuts may be added. Either vanilla sugar or cinnamon sugar is good

sprinkled on top. Can be baked in a 9″ square pan
too. Up to you.

ETHEL'S HOLIDAY SPICE CAKE

    1 cup sun-dried raisins
    2 cups water
Boil gently together until reduced to 1 cup. Cool.

Cream together thoroughly and set aside:
    ½ cup salt-free margarine, room temperature
    1 cup granulated sugar
    1 egg, room temperature, well beaten
    ¾ teaspoon maple extract
    ½ teaspoon vanilla extract

Preheat oven 350°.
In a large bowl put:
    2 cups all-purpose flour
    ½ teaspoon potassium bicarbonate
    1½ teaspoons low sodium baking powder
    ½ teaspoon nutmeg (freshly grated is grand)
    ½ teaspoon cinnamon
    ¼ teaspoon cloves—scant measure

Blend these dry ingredients well.

Add the cooled raisins to the creamed mixture you set
aside. If you omit raisins, gradually add dry mix to
creamed mix, beating vigorously after each addition.
Pour into a 9″ sprayed non-stick tube pan. Sprinkle
top with vanilla sugar (see recipe, page 115) and

bake 40-50 minutes. Does well frozen or refrigerated. *Hint:* For that old-time holiday specialty, steam this to piping hot, serve with hard sauce or foamy hot sauce, and presto—Plum Pudding!

Cookies

ICEBOX NUT OR FRUIT COOKIES

1 cup salt-free margarine
2 cups light brown sugar
2 eggs, room temperature
3½ cups all-purpose flour
1 teaspoon potassium bicarbonate
1½ teaspoons vanilla extract
1 cup chopped walnuts or sun-dried fruit

Cream margarine with sugar. Add eggs singly, stirring well with each addition. Combine flour and potassium bicarbonate, add to mixture about ⅓ at a time. When thoroughly blended, add nuts or fruit. Shape into 3 or 4 fat sausage rolls, wrap in foil or wax paper. Refrigerate overnight. Next day, the cold dough will cut readily into thin slices. Preheat oven 375°. Arrange slices on greased non-stick cookie sheet. Bake 10-12 minutes. Makes 90-100 small cookies.

Hint: Bake one "roll," sliced. Freeze the other uncooked ones in freezer wrap. It takes little more than 5 minutes to defrost enough to slice thinly while you preheat the oven. Nice to know fresh cookies are available on short notice.

MELT-AWAY BARS

1 cup salt-free margarine
1 cup vanilla sugar (see recipe, p. 115)
1 egg, room temperature and separated
1 teaspoon (generous) vanilla extract
2 cups all-purpose flour
1 cup unsalted walnuts, chopped

Preheat oven 350°.
In large mixing bowl combine margarine, sugar, egg yolk, vanilla extract, flour, and ½ cup chopped nuts. Stir thoroughly. Spread in ungreased 10″ x 15″ pan—the kind made for a jelly roll. With wire whisk, beat egg white until light and frothy. Cover pan mixture with this, sprinkle on about 2 tablespoons granulated sugar. Top with remaining ½ cup chopped nuts. Bake 25-30 minutes, or until a pleasing brown. Put pan on heat-proof surface 20 minutes or longer. Cut into bars by slicing through to bottom of pan, first lengthwise then across. Space cutting according to size you prefer. I make about 40.

Hint: If chopped nuts aren't to your liking they may be omitted from any recipe here. Substitute chopped sun-dried fruit or top with shredded coconut.

LARRY'S LEMON SQUARES

First step
Preheat oven 350°. Blend until the consistency of corn meal:

   1 cup all-purpose flour
   ½ cup salt-free margarine, room temperature
   ¼ cup confectioner's sugar

Press evenly into ungreased 8″ square pan. Bake 20 minutes. While this is cooking proceed during last five minutes with:

Second step
Beat thoroughly:

   2 eggs, room temperature
   1 cup granulated sugar
   1 teaspoon low sodium baking powder
   3 tablespoons fresh lemon juice and grated rind

When first mixture comes out of oven, pour second one over it. Return to oven, bake another 25 minutes or longer—when your finger makes no imprint, it's done. Has to "set." This must cool completely before cutting since the squares will be like lemon pie. While still in the pan, cut (as you would for brownies) into 16 squares. Store in refrigerator.

SPICY FRUIT-NUT BARS

½ cup salt-free margarine, room temperature
1 cup granulated sugar
2 teaspoons vanilla extract
1 cup sweetened applesauce
2 cups all-purpose flour
1 teaspoon potassium bicarbonate
1 teaspoon nutmeg (I prefer fresh-ground)
1½ teaspoon cinnamon

⅛ teaspoon cloves
1 cup sun-dried raisins
¼ cup unsalted walnuts, chopped (omit if you wish)

Preheat oven 350°.
Cream together margarine, sugar, and vanilla. Stir in applesauce. Blend flour with potassium bicarbonate before mixing into creamed mixture. Add other flavorings, beat thoroughly. Lace in raisins and the optional walnuts. Spread into greased and floured 10″ x 15″ cookie tin that has sides. Before baking, make a topping of ⅛ cup *light* brown sugar and 1 teaspoon cinnamon. Sprinkle this atop the dough. Bake 15 minutes. Check, then go another 5 minutes if needed. Leave in pan to cool. Cut into "fingers" or bars, triangles, squares, preferably fairly small. Store in a cool place.

OLD-FASHIONED SUGAR WAFERS

1 cup vanilla sugar (see recipe, p. 115)
1 cup salt-free margarine (2 sticks)
1 egg, room temperature
1 teaspoon vanilla or almond extract *or* ½ teaspoon each
2½ cups all-purpose flour

Cream sugar, margarine, and your choice of above flavorings until light and unified. Add egg and blend. Pour in flour gradually—⅛ at a time—as you continue beating. Shape mixture into patties, like hamburgers, about ½″ thick and 4″ across. Wrap each in foil and refrigerate overnight. (See hint below.) Next day place one patty at a time on a bread board sprinkled with vanilla sugar instead of flour. Preheat oven 375°. Sprinkle top of patty with vanilla sugar, then roll to thickness desired. Cut into squares, rectangles, triangles, or use fancy cookie cutters. Bake on non-stick cookie sheet 10-12 minutes or until a toasty gold. They're ready sooner than expected so watch carefully. Each patty makes between 12 and 18, depending on how thinly dough is rolled out.

Hints: 1. As with the ice box cookies, these patties may be frozen and then used on short notice. Let dough defrost 5 minutes before rolling.

2. Before baking, top cookies with different mixtures—cinnamon sugar, colored sugars, etc.

COUSIN DOT'S SPOON-DROPS

    1 stick salt-free margarine, room temperature
    ⅓ cup vanilla sugar (see recipe, p. 115)
    ¾ cup all-purpose flour, sifted
    1 egg, room temperature and well beaten
    1 teaspoon vanilla or almond extract *or*
       ½ teaspoon each

Preheat oven 350°.
Cream margarine, sugar, and flavoring. Stir in beaten egg. Add flour gradually, mixing all along. Spacing well apart, drop small dollops of mixture onto non-stick sprayed cookie sheet from a teaspoon. Flatten the spoon drops with bottom of a glass tumbler dipped in milk or fresh fruit juice. Sprinkle with sugar, then bake 7-10 minutes. Watch carefully lest they burn. Press very thin. Makes 35-40 depending on how thin they are. Much better very thin.

Hint: These are easy and quick enough for a child to make as a surprise—with your supervision, of course.

It's an enjoyable way to get the younger family members interested in special cookery. Try it next rainy day when time hangs heavy.

WEE FILLED DOONE TREATS

>   1 cup salt-free margarine (2 sticks, very soft)
>   ½ cup confectioner's sugar
>   2 cups all-purpose flour
>   1¾ teaspoons vanilla extract

Preheat oven 350°.

Blend all ingredients together. Pinch off a small amount, roll into a ball with hands. Place on greased cookie sheet. Flatten slightly and make depression in center with small bottle cap, thimble, or round demi spoon. Repeat for rest of dough, spacing well apart. Fill centers with your choice of jams, marmalades, jellies. Bake 15-20 minutes, checking often. Do not brown. Makes about 40-45 cookies, 2½ inches each. Size depends on the amount pinched off for them.

Variations: Make a few large enough to serve as dessert tarts filled with dollops of flavored whipped cream. Also, unfilled baked 4-inch ones are nice "shells" to dress up servings of sliced fruit or to spoon a leftover pudding into. I like to combine fruit with custard sauce (see recipe, page 98).

ONE-BOWL OATMEAL COOKIES

>   1 cup all-purpose flour
>   1 cup oatmeal, uncooked (regular, not instant)

½ cup sun-dried raisins
½ cup salt-free, margarine, melted
½ cup granulated sugar
1 egg, room temperature
½ teaspoon potassium bicarbonate
2 tablespoons Featherweight liquid milk
¼ teaspoon cinnamon
1 teaspoon vanilla extract

Preheat oven 325°.
Take a large mixing bowl and add the ingredients just as they're listed above. The only separate step is melting the margarine. Stir thoroughly. Drop by ½ teaspoonfuls onto greased cookie sheet, spacing well apart. Flatten into rounds with back of fork. Bake 15 minutes. Makes 44 2″ round cookies.

Variations: There are really four kinds of cookies that can be made from this simple mixture—plain oatmeal, with raisins, with chopped unsalted nuts, with both. Share the recipe with the family youngsters, who will have a ball filling the bowl. Double the recipe if you're on a baking spree.

COUNTRY NUT CRISPS

½ cup vegetable shortening
1 cup light brown sugar
2 teaspoons vanilla extract
1 egg, unbeaten and room temperature
1 cup all-purpose flour
¼ teaspoon potassium bicarbonate
½ cup chopped unsalted walnuts

Preheat oven 325°.
Blend shortening, sugar, and vanilla. Add egg, beat
until light and fluffy. Combine flour with potassium
bicarbonate, add to first mixture ⅛ at a time, stirring
throughout. Fold in nuts last. To arrange for baking,
take walnut-sized pieces of dough and press them flat
on a non-stick cookie sheet. They expand in cooking
so space well apart. Sprinkle each with cinnamon
sugar or vanilla sugar (see recipe, page 115). For
variety, try some with each, leave some plain. This
recipe makes 35-40 cookies, depending on how big
pressed-down dabs are. Cool on rack, store covered.

Hint: A glass tumbler dipped in water is handy for
flattening the dough.

FROSTED COOKIE LOGS

1 cup salt-free margarine, room temperature
¾ cup vanilla sugar (see recipe, p. 115)
1 teaspoon vanilla extract
1 teaspoon either lemon or almond extract
1 egg, well beaten
2½ cups all-purpose flour

Preheat oven 350°.
Cream together margarine, sugar, and flavorings. Stir
in beaten egg. Blend in flour gradually. Put unchilled
dough through cookie press—I like the star and ribbon
shapes. Space on a sprayed non-stick cookie sheet and
bake 8-10 minutes until golden. Cool and cut into 2"
or 3" lengths. Top each with your favorite frosting
(omit salt from recipe) by using a press to draw a thin
beading down each. Makes about 40-50 delicate logs

with a decidedly continental flair. Guests really go for these so don't let the quantity stop you.

Hint: I make a simple mocha frosting for these, using Hershey's cocoa. Remember, Dutch-process chocolate is a no-no! The other's better for everyone, anyway.

FLORENCE'S BUTTERSCOTCH BROWNIES

4 tablespoons salt-free margarine
1 cup light brown sugar
1 egg, room temperature and beaten
¾ cup all-purpose flour
1½ teaspoons low sodium baking powder
1 teaspoon vanilla extract
¼ cup unsalted pecans or walnuts, chopped

Preheat oven 300°.
In a large saucepan, stir margarine and sugar over low heat until well blended. Remove from stove and when lukewarm add beaten egg and the combined flour and baking powder, mixing all together. Stir in vanilla extract and chopped nuts. Spread in a greased or sprayed 8″ x 8″ pan—bake 30 minutes. Cut into squares before it becomes cold.

Pastry and Pies

BASIC PASTRY

This recipe makes enough pastry for a 9″ bottom shell, a two-crust pie, and a couple of small tarts, depending on the thickness you roll out. I make the whole recipe (except for the ice water), divide it into three, use one and refrigerate the other two. When I want to make another pie or tarts, the pastry's all ready, needing only ice water and rolling.

> 1 cup vegetable shortening
> 1 tablespoon salt-free margarine
> 3 cups all-purpose flour
> 1 tablespoon granulated sugar
> ¼ cup ice water

Preheat oven 450°.
For recipe calling for ready-baked shell, blend all ingredients well, add just enough finger-sprinkled ice water to hold pastry together. Roll out with a light touch on a floured board. Fit and trim to size in pie or tart plates. Bake about 12 minutes, or until it becomes a sunny tan. Reduce heat to 350°, continue baking 15-20 minutes. Set aside to cool while you make your choice of filling or freeze for later use.

Hints: Depending on the filling's flavor, season the crust with nutmeg, cinnamon, or freshly grated lemon rind. For a two-crust pie, brush top with Featherweight liquid milk or water, sprinkle with vanilla sugar and dots of salt-free margarine before baking. This makes a handsome crunchy top.

NATURALLY APPLE PIE

For crust, use the Basic Pastry recipe (page 91), rolling out enough chilled dough to make bottom and top trimmed to an 8″ or 9″ pie plate. I sprinkle the board with vanilla sugar (see recipe, page 115), instead of flour, and flavor the pastry with a light dusting of commercial apple pie spice.

8″ or 9″ pie plate
6-7 large apples, peeled and thin-sliced
(I prefer Mac's)
⅔ cup granulated sugar
1 teaspoon nutmeg (try grating your own)
½ teaspoon cinnamon
grated rind of 1 lemon
1 tablespoon fresh lemon juice

Preheat oven 450°.
In a large bowl, blend all above ingredients—not the pie plate, of course! Fit rolled-out bottom crust loosely into pie plate with a slight overhang all around. Pile in filling from bowl, mounding it in center. Moisten trimmed edge of pastry with water, place top crust over apple mix. Seal edges by fork-edging or squeeze

with finger and thumb to merge both crusts and make
a chef-style border. Prick top with fork points or knife
slashes in a design—a family initial is fun. Dot with
salt-free margarine, sprinkle with water or Featherweight liquid milk. Top with dusting of vanilla sugar
or cinnamon sugar. This makes for a crunchy glazed
crust. Bake 10 minutes, then lower heat to 325° for
40-45 minutes. It's done when a fork pierce tells you
filling is soft. Cool before cutting.

CARRIE'S LEMON MERINGUE PIE

For crust, see Basic Pastry recipe (page 91) and
make a 9″ pie shell, with freshly grated lemon rind
added before rolling out pastry. Bake and cool before
filling.

FILLING FOR PIE SHELL

3 tablespoons cornstarch
1¼ cups granulated sugar
1 tablespoon lemon rind, grated
¼ cup fresh-squeezed lemon juice
3 eggs, room temperature, separated
1½ cups boiling water

In quart-size sauce pan, combine the first four ingredients. Beat egg yolks to a light yellow, stir into
mixture. Gradually add boiling water. Bring filling to
a boil over direct heat, stirring constantly with a whisk.
It takes about 4-5 minutes to thicken during this stirring. Pour into baked pie shell. Set aside while making:

MERINGUE TOPPING

Preheat oven 425°.
In a bowl beat the 3 egg whites till stiff, gradually adding 6 tablespoons sugar, one at a time. Spread on pie lightly, making meringue curl into peaks with a narrow rubber spatula. Be sure meringue is sealed to crust's edges. Sprinkle with sugar. Bake 3-4 minutes or until meringue is delicately toasted. Remove and put the whole triumph on a wire rack to cool. Serves 7.

MOTHER HUBBARD SQUASH PIE

1¾ cups cooked strained squash, cooled
½ cup granulated sugar
1 teaspoon powdered ginger
½ teaspoon nutmeg (I use fresh-ground)
½ teaspoon cinnamon
2 eggs, room temperature and beaten
1½ cups Featherweight liquid milk
1 unbaked pie shell in 9″ plate

Preheat oven 425°.
In a large bowl, mix sugar and spices. Blend in squash thoroughly. Stir milk into beaten eggs, add to squash mixture, and unify the whole filling. Pour into the unbaked pie shell in pie plate. Bake 20 minutes, then turn oven down to 350° or 325° and continue cooking about 40-50 minutes more. Sprinkle top with nutmeg. It's done when a thin-bladed knife inserted into center comes out clean. Cool (in pie plate) on rack.

Hint: Add several shakes of cinnamon or nutmeg (both if you like) to pie shell pastry before baking it.

Variations: Substitute pumpkin for the same amount of squash and proceed with the rest of the recipe.

For a special occasion dot the top of the pie with ¾ cup miniature marshmallows before baking.

Quick Trick: Both squash and pumpkin are available canned in amounts just right for one pie filling. Use either one instead of the cooking and straining called for above. BUT be sure to buy the brand that does not list salt in the fine print on its label.

GRANNY'S LEMON SPONGE PIE

> 1 cup granulated sugar
> 2 eggs, room temperature and separated
> 1 teaspoon corn oil
> 2 tablespoons all-purpose flour
> 1 lemon, grated rind and juice
> 1 cup Featherweight liquid milk
> 1 unbaked shell in 8″ or 9″ pie plate

Preheat oven 450°.

Mix together thoroughly: sugar, egg yolks, oil, and flour. Add lemon rind and juice. Stir in milk. Beat egg whites stiff and fold into the mixture. Pour into unbaked pie shell. Bake 10 minutes, reduce heat to 325°-350° and continue cooking 35 minutes or until a thin metal knife comes out clean. Cool before cutting this pie, which ends up with its own sponge top on a custard base. Serves 6-7.

Variation: If you're counting calories (and who isn't?) try this filling as a dessert custard. Fill 5½-ounce oven-proof glass cups with mixture and bake as directed above. Omitting the pastry makes the calories crash. But have it as a pie sometimes, too.

Puddings

NONIE'S CUSTARD BREAD PUDDING
with self-made sauce

3 slices salt-free bread, with crusts trimmed
2 cups Featherweight liquid milk
2 eggs (3 if small), room temperature
1½ teaspoons vanilla extract
1 cup light brown sugar

Spread bread with salt-free margarine. Cut slices into small cubes. Put sugar into top of double boiler, add bread cubes. In a bowl, beat eggs, milk, and vanilla. Pour this over bread-sugar mix but do NOT stir. Put atop gently boiling water in bottom of double boiler and cook, covered, 1-1½ hours or until a thin knife inserted in center of custard comes out clean. Serve warm or chilled in individual dessert dishes, spooning on the sauce you'll discover at the bottom of the pan under the cooked custard.

Hint: Don't discard bread crusts from salt-free loaves. File them away in a plastic bag in your freezer. When enough accumulate, you have the basis for splendid poultry stuffing. Add your own selection of sage, thyme, onion, mushrooms, chopped nuts, a few oysters —whatever you like that is salt-free. Experiment and you'll come up with a personal prize.

BAMPY'S LEMON SNOW
with custard sauce

2 tablespoons (2 packages) granulated
    plain gelatin
1 cup cold water
2 cups boiling water
2 lemons—grated rind and juice
1 cup granulated sugar
2 eggs, room temperature and separated

Sprinkle gelatin over cold water. Let stand 10 minutes.
Pour in boiling water, stir well, and cool. Add juice,
grated lemon rind, and mix sugar in, stirring until dissolved. Cool until thickened. Then whip mixture well.
Beat egg whites stiff, fold into gelatin. Refrigerate to
set. Makes one quart.

CUSTARD SAUCE

2 egg yolks—from eggs used above
2 cups Featherweight liquid milk
¼ cup granulated sugar
1½″ slice of vanilla bean

Beat egg yolks in top of double boiler. Add milk and
sugar. Blend. Split slice of vanilla bean, scrape lining
into mix, add shell pieces. Cook over medium heat
until custard coats a spoon well. Fish out the vanilla
bean shell. If you wish, add vanilla extract to taste.
Refrigerate. Makes one pint.

To serve, pour sauce over mounds of lemon snow in
dessert dishes. Or, if you have a pet crystal compote,

pour in the sauce, float the snow mounds in it and ladle it out at the table—a marvelously edible landscape!

Hint: Use leftover custard sauce on fruit cup or slices of spice cake. I like it on coffee gelatin (See pages 79 and 116 for spice cake and coffee gelatin recipes.)

Variation: Try fresh orange juice and grated rind in place of the lemon. Quick-change artist!

BUFFY'S ORANGE-BANANA CREAM

⅓ cup Featherweight *dry* milk
2 cups water
⅓ cup vanilla sugar
2 tablespoons corn starch, level measure
1 egg, room temperature and beaten
1½″ slice of vanilla bean
3 oranges
1 large banana (or 2 small)

In a 1-quart saucepan, stir together milk and water until smooth. Add sugar, corn starch, and egg. Split vanilla bean, scrape center into mixture, toss in the split shell, and stir. Let stand while you prepare fruit. Into a bowl, cut up peeled sections of orange (with juice) and banana, sprinkling with granulated sugar to taste, and set aside to melt. Meanwhile, back at the old stove, turn heat to medium, cook mixture in saucepan until thickened—about 10 minutes—stirring constantly as it boils gently. If it begins to stick, lower heat lest it scorch. When thick enough, fish out the vanilla bean shell, fold into fruit, and chill thoroughly.

Makes 6-8 servings which will be lapped up and purred over.

Hint: 2 cups Featherweight *liquid* milk can be used instead of the first two ingredients above. I listed the dry in case you're rushed and have none pre-mixed. Results are the same, convenience isn't.

Variations: Canned (read that label!) or fresh peaches, cherries, berries in any combination your family's tastes dictate, can be used as well as orange and banana. Use half of the custard recipe for a cream puff filling (see recipe, page 110). Fold in 2 tablespoons cream whipped with vanilla sugar flavoring. That amount of cream is permissible.

FOAMY TAPIOCA CREME

3 tablespoons vanilla sugar (see recipe, p. 115)
3 tablespoons *dry* tapioca
2 cups Featherweight liquid milk
1 egg, room temperature and separated
1½″ slice of vanilla bean
2 tablespoons sugar

In a large saucepan, mix together sugar, tapioca, milk, egg yolk. Add scrapings from inside of vanilla bean and the two pieces of shell. Let stand about 45 minutes. While waiting, beat egg white until stiff, adding 2 tablespoons of sugar, one at a time. Set aside. Cook saucepan mixture over medium heat for 10-15 minutes, stirring constantly with wire whisk until thickened and glossy. Remove pieces of vanilla bean shell. Remove from heat, fold beaten egg white into tapioca, and test for flavor. If you prefer a more enhanced taste, add a few drops of vanilla extract and sample it. Fold again after 30 minutes, cover, and refrigerate. Before serving, take a few folding turns with a large spoon, then ladle the Foamy Creme into dessert cups or, for a whimsical note, into wide wine glasses!

Variation: For a crowning touch, pop a huge fresh strawberry atop each serving, or any other pampered fruit you choose. Mandarin oranges? It's not reckless to add a heaping teaspoon of whipped cream, either!

EASY STEAMED CUSTARDS

 3 eggs, room temperature
 3 cups Featherweight liquid milk
 ⅛ cup vanilla sugar (see recipe, p. 115)
 1 teaspoon vanilla extract
 nutmeg for topping

Set out seven 5-ounce heat-proof custard cups. Beat eggs slightly, add milk, sugar, and vanilla. Blend thoroughly. Pour into cups, top each with a grating of nutmeg. Cook in either an electric frying pan (if you have a 10″ or 12″ one), *or* a baking pan.

For Electric Fry Pan: Fill pan halfway up with water. Heat to 320°. When boiling, turn to 200°, place filled cups in water, cover, and cook 45-60 minutes. Test by inserting a thin knife blade. Custard is done when knife comes out clean.

For Oven Baking Pan: Fill pan ¾″ deep with warm water. Heat in 350° oven to boiling. Reduce to 250°. Place filled cups in water. Poach 45-60 minutes, uncovered. Test as for electric pan method. Remove cups to cake rack to cool, then refrigerate. Extra good with a topping of pure maple syrup.

Hint: With either method, do not allow water to boil or evaporate once the custard cups are in it. Reduce heat to keep a steady low simmer, and add hot tap water as needed. This steamed custard is more delicate and tender than a baked one, thus providing a change in texture and taste.

Salad Days

SALAD FRUITS, VEGETABLES & GREENS
With a Choice of Gourmet Garnishments

Go easy on the lettuce leaves, using them mostly for background accents. Besides, it's really dull to pad a salad with lettuce when you have this green-light list. Try any of these items in whatever combinations your family's tastes dictate. Variety is intriguing and pays off.

Aside from salads, there are some bonus ideas for dips and appetizers here. Think of slicing in two different ways: Cut cucumber across for salads, lengthwise into sturdy sticks for munching. Same for any raw vegetable listed here. The salad dressings can be thickened for dips.

SALAD FRUITS, VEGETABLES

> Apple—nice chopped with nuts
> Apricot—fresh or canned
> Asparagus—fresh or canned
> Avocado—½ small
> Banana
> Beans—raw, cooked, canned no-salt
>   green
>   lima (not canned)
>   snap
>   yellow

Berries—all in season O.K.
Cabbage—raw for slaw
Cauliflower—raw or cooked
Cherries—fresh or canned
Corn—fresh or salt-controlled brand
Cucumber
Dill—fresh or dried
Fruit Cocktail—read that label!
Grapes
Grapefruit
Leeks
Mint—fresh or dried
Nectarine
Onion—sliced, diced fresh
   Bermuda
   pearl
   Spanish
Orange—all kinds
Peach—fresh or diet pack
Peas—fresh, salt-free canned
Pears—fresh, salt-free canned
Pepper—fresh, frozen
   chili
   green
   Italian
Pineapple—fresh or canned
Pimiento—water-pack
Plum—fresh or canned
Pomegranate
Potato—cooked, sliced
Radish
Scallion
Squash—sliced, diced
   summer
   zucchini
Tangelo

Tangerine
Tomato
"Ugli"

CRISPY GREENS

Cabbage, Chinese (small amounts)
Chicory
Endive
Lettuce—all varieties

GOURMET GARNISHES

Kumquat—sliced or quartered
Melon—a few thin slices
Parsley—fresh
Raisins—sun-dried only
Watercress
Nuts—unsalted, chopped
    Brazil
    filberts
    pecans
    walnuts

KITCHEN GARDEN DRESSING

1 cup (scant) granulated sugar
1 teaspoon dry mustard
2 tablespoons (level) all-purpose flour
1 egg, beaten
1½ cups water
½ cup cider vinegar

In a 1-quart saucepan, blend first three ingredients.
Whisk in the others, cook over medium heat about 10

minutes, stirring until thickened. Refrigerate in a 1-quart jar. This has an elusive sweet-sour taste that perks up any garden salad from a simple tomato-cucumber combination to the fanciest garnished medley.

HESTER'S FRENCH-STYLE DRESSING

⅓ cup low-sodium catsup
¼ cup corn oil
½ cup (scant) granulated sugar—
or to taste
juice of 1 fresh lemon
¼ medium onion, grated
¼ teaspoon ground pepper
½ cup cider vinegar

Combine all but vinegar and shake thoroughly in 1-pint container. Add the vinegar, shake vigorously, and refrigerate for a couple of days. This melds the flavors nicely. Shake before each use, of course.

This makes an unusual overnight marinade for any meat or fish, and I use it for basting, too. It can also be used to marinate leftover vegetables, for a dinner party's first course antipasto, hors d'oeuvres, or smorgasbord—choose any language, it's simply a matter of whim.

AUNT EMMA'S BOIL-UP DRESSING
with variations

2 tablespoons granulated sugar
1 teaspoon dry mustard

2 tablespoons (level) all-purpose flour
1 egg, beaten
¼ cup cider vinegar
¾ cup Featherweight liquid milk

Combine first three ingredients in a 1-quart saucepan.
Blend egg, vinegar, and milk in a bowl, add to saucepan. Mix together with a whisk and continue stirring
over medium heat until thickened, about 10 minutes.
Refrigerate in 1-pint container.

Variations:
1. If you prefer a thinner dressing, spoon out a few
ounces into a measuring cup, add as much cold
Featherweight liquid milk as you choose and stir to
consistency desired. A good way to stretch the last of
the basic batch, too.
2. A generous tablespoon of cream, whipped and then
folded into this dressing makes a unique topping for
fruit salad. It's a frosty-looking touch in summer, and,
come to think of it, fresh fruit is a dandy pick-up for
the winter doldrums. See Salad Fruits list on pages
103–05.

3. *Thousand Island Dressing:*

1 cup Aunt Emma's Boil-Up Dressing
2 tablespoons low sodium chili sauce
1 tablespoon chopped green pepper
1 tablespoon minced onion, chive, or scallion

Blend all together and chill before spooning over salad.
This recipe is literally custom-made as a guest-worthy
sauce for fish, too.

4. Russian Dressing:

To 1 cup Aunt Emma's Boil-Up Dressing, add ⅓ cup low sodium chili sauce, drained, or ⅓ cup low sodium catsup.

5. Using the boil-up recipe as a base, any choice of herbs, spices, minced garnishes (see Salad Fruits, Vegetables on pages 103–05) can be worked out as additions. Use cold Featherweight liquid milk to thin it down, dried chopped items (chives, for instance) to thicken it. The juice from salt-free cocktail onions, used instead of milk, will turn it into a party dip, with any additions you wish. It can be thin enough to merely flavor, or fluffy thick for a sandwich spread.

Miscellaneous Marvels

DEBBIE'S FILLED CREAM PUFFS

½ cup water
½ stick salt-free margarine
½ cup flour
2 eggs, room temperature

Preheat oven 450°.
In a 1-quart saucepan, bring water and margarine to a boil. Remove from stove and add flour all at once. Blend thoroughly. Add eggs singly, beating well after each addition. Continue beating until batter is glossy. Drop scant tablespoons of batter on greased baking sheet, but do not pat puffs down. Bake 10 minutes. Reduce heat to 325°, bake another 30 minutes. This amount makes 13-14 small puffs. To serve, cut off tops, fill centers with sweetened whipped cream, whole fruit preserves, or the following custard filling. Set tops back on and serve plain or with your favorite glaze or frosting drizzled over them.

Hint: To test cream puffs, remove one at end of baking time. If it deflates somewhat, return it to oven and bake 3-5 minutes longer. Ovens vary, so timing is approximate.

CUSTARD FILLING

    2 eggs
    2 teaspoons (rounded) corn starch
    2 cups Featherweight liquid milk
    ⅓ cup vanilla sugar (see recipe, p. 115)
    1½" vanilla bean

In a 1-quart saucepan, beat eggs, add cornstarch, stir
in milk and sugar. Split piece of vanilla bean, scrape
center out into pan, add shell. Blend mixture until
completely smooth. Bring to a boil over medium heat,
stirring constantly with a whisk. It will thicken in about
10 minutes. Remove vanilla bean shell. Remove from
heat and cool. Add more flavoring if desired. Fill puffs
as directed. Chill before serving.
Note: 1 egg may be used if you must watch cholesterol
levels, but do not use egg substitutes.

PIQUANT MEAT SAUCE

    3 tablespoons light brown sugar
    4 tablespoons low sodium catsup
    ¼ teaspoon nutmeg (fresh-ground is best)
    1 teaspoon dry mustard

If you're an onion buff, add as much of it minced as
you wish—or scallion, chive, shallot, whichever's
handy. Mix well and refrigerate in a covered jar. It's a
taste-tingling accompaniment for cold meats and I use
it when preparing economy beef dishes:

For meat loaf: Spread mixture on top before baking,
    then cook as usual.

For hamburgers: Shape and broil them on one side, turn, plop a good tablespoon of the sauce on top, and return to broiler until done.

For canape meat balls: Mix ground meat with some of the sauce, shape into small balls, and broil. Thin sauce with basic Aunt Emma's Boil-Up Salad Dressing, serve in a dip bowl with meat balls and cocktail picks.

UP-COUNTRY ORCHARD APPLESAUCE

It's plain silly to write out a formal recipe for this, but while store-bought applesauce is perfectly all right, I'd just like to persuade you to make your own for the whole family's enjoyment. Children are wide-eyed watching the quick and simple process, someone invariably wants a prompt answer to "What smells so fantastic?"—and there's a real satisfaction in the nostalgic idea of such a foolproof bit of kitchen heritage.

Six big apples will make a generous quart. Peel, core, and cut them into a saucepan. Add water about half way up. Sprinkle in some cinnamon, ground clove, sugar, and fresh lemon juice; add a touch of allspice if you wish. Don't overspice; you can always add more later when tasting. Bring to a boil and after a minute or two start squishing it up with a wire whisk. I prefer it chunky. If you don't, simply whisk it vigorously. No prescribed ingredients or timing, so call it your own private recipe!

Like Pink Applesauce? Boil the peeled skins first, strain the colored juice, and cook the cut-up apples in that. Or if you like shortcuts, just sneak in a couple of drops of red coloring instead. Refrigerate the apple-sauce in a screw-top jar or freeze small portions.

Hint: This makes a nice gift for the small fry on your list. Save screw-top jars and dress them up with labels on which you can write the child's name. Or decorate with a decal or nail polish.

CINNAMON APPLE CRUNCH

If your childhood memories include a whiff of Brown Betty, reminisce no more. Here's that old favorite in a new quick-and-easy form. Only time and extra washing up are eliminated, not the flavor or texture.

> 5 medium-size apples
> ⅓ cup orange juice
> ¼ cup granulated sugar
> ½ cup light brown sugar
> ¾ teaspoon cinnamon
> ¾ cup all-purpose flour
> ¼ cup (½ stick) salt-free margarine

Preheat oven 375°.
Peel, core, and thickly slice (about ½") enough apples to make six cups. Turn these into either an 8" square baking pan or low 2-quart baking dish, well greased. Combine granulated sugar with orange juice, pour over apple slices. Cream margarine, cinnamon, and light brown sugar together, then add flour, blending gradually with mixing fork until it's all an even crumbly texture. Spoon this over the apple mixture. Bake until the topping is browned well but not mushy.

Takes about 40 minutes, but set the timer for 35, just to check.

Variation: Instead of orange juice, try commercial apricot nectar. Either provides a refreshing change from the sometimes overly sweet taste of Brown Betty.

Hints: This can be served in individual dishes either warm or cold. I like it with a topping of chilled Featherweight liquid milk; my husband prefers whipped cream or a not-quite-hard sauce made with whipped salt-free margarine, sugar, and vanilla extract.

GERRY'S PANCAKES

- 1 cup all-purpose flour (extra-fine is better)
- 2 teaspoons, slightly rounded, low sodium baking powder
- 3 generous tablespoons granulated sugar
- 1 egg, room temperature
- ¾ cup Featherweight liquid milk
- 2 tablespoons corn oil

In a 1-quart measuring pitcher, blend flour and baking powder. Separately beat together egg, milk, oil. Stir into first mixture. (The amount of milk depends on how thick you like pancakes to be, so try a couple this way, then add more milk to batter if desired.) Stir well as you proceed.

For Electric Fry Pan: Preheat to 380°. Spray or oil surface. Pour a small amount of batter in each corner of pan—it'll spread. When bubbles form on top, turn cakes and cook until both sides are toasty brown.

For Stove-Top Fry Pan: Follow same process as above, but preheat non-stick fry pan over medium heat, depending on your stove's own quirks. I've learned each is different *and* at different times of the year. Have the pan hot enough without producing a smoke screen.

Measure about ¼ cup batter for each pancake. To serve, have warm plates ready. Stack pancakes in serving portions and expect them to disappear fast. Serve with pure maple syrup and whipped salt-free margarine (see recipe below).

Variation: For dessert pancakes with a French accent, thin batter with Featherweight liquid milk until batter makes lacy golden-brown edible "doilies" delicate enough to roll up. Allow three to a serving. Reheat crepes. Serve with a sauce made from your favorite marmalade, melted salt-free margarine, sugar, and a dash of rum or brandy extract. Or sprinkle with sugar, omitting flavoring extract.

Makes 16 pancakes and almost double that for crepes.

WHIPPED SALT-FREE MARGARINE

For a lighter accompaniment to hot muffins and breads, pancakes, or just for a texture change, this is simplicity itself to make. In electric blender put ½ cup room temperature salt-free margarine and ¼ cup Featherweight liquid milk. Blend until all liquid is absorbed. Store in a pretty little glass or china crock with a top. Chill until firm. Serve from the crock.

Variations: For a hint of hollandaise, use half milk, half fresh lemon juice and use on asparagus, broccoli, green beans, broiled fish, or what have you. As with the salad dressing variations in these pages, try adding minced parsley, scallion—play to your heart's (and appetite's) content, inventing any number of pretty palatables. Try confectioner's sugar and vanilla extract with the basic recipe and you will have a fluffy sauce for either of the spice cakes in this collection or any recipe using apples.

CANDY BOX DATES

Start with a package of pitted sun-dried dates. Split fruit lengthwise with a sharp knife. Stuff each section with your choice of salt-free nuts (either chopped or whole), low sodium peanut butter, or marshmallow bits. Press dates together again. Roll in plain granulated or vanilla sugar (see recipe below) and refrigerate to set.

Hint: For an even coating and a speedy no-mess job of it, put the sugar in a plastic bag, pop the dates in a few at a time, and shake 'em up. I'm all for these pampering shortcuts.

An assortment of the stuffed dates and a sampling of our cookies makes an especially thoughtful gift idea for holiday hostesses and hearty snackers.

VANILLA SUGAR

A vanilla bean is the magic wand that turns ordinary granulated sugar into a prized ingredient. Available in most spice departments, the dreary appearance of this long limp bean belies its sorcery.

To make vanilla sugar, put one pound granulated sugar into a container which has a tight-fitting lid. Split one vanilla bean, scrape out the inside, mix scrapings with sugar. Insert the beans' split shell into center, cover, and store at least one week. The longer it stands, the better the flavor.

I use vanilla sugar in so many recipes, as you'll soon notice in reading through these pages. When the supply is down to about half, mix up another batch and let that age while you're using up the first. It keeps indefinitely, gaining more of its unique flavor as the weeks go by.

JANICE'S COFFEE GELATIN

2 tablespoons granulated gelatin, plain
½ cup cold water
1 cup boiling water in pan
⅓ cup granulated sugar
2 cups boiled coffee

Soak gelatin in cold water about 5 minutes, then dissolve by stirring into boiling water. Add sugar, blend in coffee. Pour into a 4-cup mold, individual molds, or dessert compotes. Chill until set—about 3 hours. Serves 5. Serve with 2 tablespoons cream whipped fluffy with vanilla sugar. (As we have explained earlier, the sodium in fresh cream is so minor it doesn't even count.)

MY GELATIN SAMPLER

Since there is a limited number of flavors in the special low sodium packaged gelatin, I do my own variations. As with fashion accessories, I like to "mix and match" gelatin flavors, uses and effects. Some make sparkling salad molds—individual ones, buffet supper rings, family reunion platters. Wine gelatins look festive served, of course, in wine glasses. Do try any of these, both for two *and* company.

I cut down on the sugar if the flavoring liquid is particularly sweet. Salad aspics need more lemon juice than sugar—unless it's a fruit salad. Just taste as you go along and, like me, you'll arrive at what pleases all the family best.

Take a look at this list—and be sure to read labels on cans, bottles, frozen foods. Salt? Sodium? Skip it. Look for other brands in diet and gourmet sections at your market.

Apple cider

Apricot nectar

Berry juices

Cocoa—not Dutch process

Fish stock—boiled down, strained

Fruit punch

Fruit wine

Grape juice—red or white

Grapefruit juice

Lemon—fresh squeezed, strained

Lime—fresh squeezed, strained

Mint—diluted sauce

Mocha—half cocoa, half coffee

Muscatel—see below

Orange—fresh squeezed, strained

Pineapple—canned only

Port—see below

Rhubarb—syrup

Sherry—see below

Tomato juice—dietetic only

For exact proportions, you'll find recipe folders in the packages of unflavored gelatin. Merely vary these recipes for whatever ingredients you choose, keeping the basic balance of liquid to gelatin to make sure the mixture will set.

About wine gelatins: As a general guide, add ⅛ cup strained orange juice and 3 tablespoons strained lemon juice to 1 cup dry sherry or other dry wine. Reverse the proportions of fruit juice for a sweet wine such as port or muscatel, adding more lemon than orange juice. Adjust to your own taste, keeping the total liquid measurements in line for any basic gelatin recipe. For a triumph of a dessert, pour wine gelatin into a ring mold which you've rinsed in cold water. When it's chilled and set, unmold onto a cold platter. Fill center with sweetened cut-up fruit and serve it at the table. Candlelight is a must!

Tomato juice and fish stock make a good duo for an aspic. Add finely chopped cucumber to your choice of salad dressings (see recipes) as an accompaniment to the aspic. Use chicken stock for an aspic to accompany cold sliced turkey. Or put diced poultry meat right into gelatin—this is a surprise disguise for leftover meat in party dress. Individual molds are easy: fill those oven-proof glass custard cups, refrigerate until set, then unmold right onto the salad of luncheon plates you'll use at the table.

WHIPPED CREAM AND VARIATIONS

Aside from the standard formula (2 tablespoons sugar and 1 teaspoon vanilla extract to 1 cup of cream, whipped), there are many delightful variations on the theme of cream. Once it is whipped into stiff peaks, add your choice of these ideas and then go on to dream up your own.

❈

Beat in ¼ cup strained fresh fruit such as berries or peaches. Add sugar to taste.

❈

Beat in 2 tablespoonfuls orange liqueur, creme de cacao, or any other cordial you like. Creme de menthe whipped cream is marvelous on lime gelatin, as is Kahlua-flavored whipped cream on coffee gelatin.

❈

Fold in 2 tablespoons sugar, 2 tablespoons strained lemon juice, and a generous grating of lemon rind for a New Orleans touch.

❈

For holiday toppings, add food coloring drop by drop to the standard formula: beat in green for St. Patrick's Day, red for a Valentine's pink, but do avoid blue because it looks too much like roquefort cheese spread!

❈

Use any extract such as peppermint, maple, rum, instead of vanilla, depending on what the whipped cream is used with.

❈

Instead of the standard recipe, I prefer to use vanilla sugar along with vanilla extract.

APPENDIX

BREADS

		Milligrams Sodium	Milligrams Potassium	Grams Carbohydrate	Grams Fat	Grams Protein	Calories
DAVID'S DATE NUT BREAD							
5" & 9" loaf pan	TOTAL	113	1651	476	45	37	2460
18 slices	1 slice	6	92	25	2	2	137
20 slices	1 slice	5	83	24	2	2	123
GLAZED ORANGE BREAD							
9" x 5" loaf pan	TOTAL	170	1112	562	136	53	3685
18 slices	1 slice	9	62	31	7	6	205
DOUBLE-DUTY CORN BREAD							
8" x 8" pan	TOTAL	136	314	333	56	47	2029
9 squares	1 square	15	35	37	6	5	225
16 slices 1" x 4"	1 slice	9	20	21	3	3	127
32 slices 1/2" x 4"	1 slice	4	10	11	2	1	63
CLAIRE'S LEMON DESSERT BREAD							
5" x 9" loaf pan	TOTAL	132	279	333	112	35	2481
glaze	TOTAL	1	3	108	—	1	436
bread & glaze	TOTAL	133	282	441	112	36	2917
18 slices	1 slice	7	16	25	6	2	162
20 slices	1 slice	6	14	22	5	2	146

BREADS (cont.)

	Milligrams Sodium	Milligrams Potassium	Grams Carbohydrate	Grams Fat	Grams Protein	Calories
MOTHER'S ENGLISH TEA LOAF						
2 loaves	23	979	366	32	42	1956
1 loaf	13	490	183	16	21	978
FRECKLED BANANA BREAD						
9" x 5" loaf pan TOTAL	69	1687	401	100	22	2615
20 slices — 1 slice	3	84	20	5	1	131
+ ½ cup walnuts TOTAL	1	225	8	32	12	325
FERN LODGE MUFFINS						
12 muffins TOTAL	81	277	247	38	38	1479
1 muffin TOTAL	7	23	20	3	3	126
POPOVERS ARE PUSHOVERS						
6 - 5½ oz. custard cups TOTAL	131	235	96	11	34	616
	22	39	16	2	5	101
APRIL FOOL'S GINGERBREAD						
18 cup cakes TOTAL	84	439	457	106	28	2901
1 cup cakes	5	24	25	6	2	161
8" x 8" pan - 9 squares — 1 square	9	49	51	12	3	322
CAKES						
FATHER'S FAVORITE SPONGE CAKE						
16 servings TOTAL	132	231	284	11	25	1339
1 slice	9	14	18	1	¾	84
9 squares — 1 square	15	24	32	3	1	149

CAKES (cont.)

		Calories	Grams Protein	Grams Fat	Grams Carbohydrate	Milligrams Potassium	Milligrams Sodium
AUNT JEANIE'S APPLESAUCE CAKE							
5" x 9" loaf pan	TOTAL	2826	8	93	489	1490	62
16 slices	1 slice	177	½	6	31	93	4
KAY'S NO-CHEATING CHOCOLATE CAKE							
8" x 8" pan	TOTAL	2175	11	90	329	499	5
16 slices - no frosting	1 serving	136	1	6	11	31	3
9 squares - no frosting	1 serving	242	1	10	37	55	½
16 slices with frosting (1 egg white)	1 serving	94	½	3	17	18	3
9 squares with frosting	1 serving	16T	1	5	30	33	6
ALMA'S SOUR CREAM SPICE CAKE							
	TOTAL	3353	41	147	466	1204	309
18 slices	1 slice	185	2	8	26	67	17
20 slices	1 slice	167	2	7	23	60	15
ETHEL'S HOLIDAY SPICE CAKE							
10" tube pan	TOTAL	2916	34	97	476	1502	123
16 slices	1 slice	182	2	6	30	94	8
COOKIES							
ICE BOX NUT OR FRUIT COOKIES							
approx. 100 cookies (small)	TOTAL	5499	72	260	724	2488	286
	1 cookie	55	1	2	7	25	3

COOKIES (cont.)

		Milligrams Sodium	Milligrams Potassium	Grams Carbohydrate	Grams Fat	Grams Protein	Calories
MELT-AWAY BARS 10" x 15" pan							
	TOTAL	91	731	384	255	47	4017
	1 log	2	18	10	6	1	100
	1 log	2	15	8	5	1	80
LARRY'S LEMON SQUARES 8" x 8" square pan							
16 squares	TOTAL	138	323	320	104	26	2318
	1 square	8	20	20	7	142	145
SPICY FRUIT-NUT BARS 10" x 15" cookie sheet with sides (minus nuts)							
50 logs	TOTAL	66	1603	561	94	28	3202
	1 log	1	32	11	2	½	64
OLD-FASHIONED SUGAR WAFERS number depends on size of cookie	TOTAL	105	380	469	210	14	3822
COUSIN DOT'S SPOON DROPS small batch	TOTAL	748	155	148	105	15	2580
WEE FILLED DOOME TREATS	TOTAL	39	254	254	199	63	3057

COOKIES (cont.)

		Milligrams Sodium	Milligrams Potassium	Grams Carbohydrate	Grams Fat	Grams Protein	Calories
ONE-BOWL OATMEAL COOKIES							
44 cookies	TOTAL	96	783	319	96	47	2328
	1 cookie	2	18	7	2	1	53
COUNTRY NUT CRISPS	TOTAL	130	1152	304	155	26	2715
35 cookies	1 cookie	3	33	8	4	2	78
40 cookies	1 cookie	3	29	7	4	1	68
FROSTED COOKIE LOGS	TOTAL	88	385	360	192	36	3312
10" x 15" cookie sheet	1 strip	2	8	7	4	1	66
FLORENCE'S BUTTERSCOTCH BROWNIES	TOTAL	138	1010	278	22	21	1394
8" x 8" pan (16 squares)	1 square	9	63	17	1	1	87

PASTRY AND PIES

		Milligrams Sodium	Milligrams Potassium	Grams Carbohydrate	Grams Fat	Grams Protein	Calories
PASTRY (Basic Mixture)	TOTAL	7	315	264	248	34	3430
divide into thirds	1 pie shell	2	105	88	82	11	1143
double crust		4	210	176	165	22	2286

PASTRY AND PIES (cont.)

		Sodium Milligrams	Potassium Milligrams	Carbohydrate Grams	Fat Grams	Protein Grams	Calories
NATURALLY APPLE PIE 9" pie plate	TOTAL	18	1371	53	172	26	3754
cut into 7 pieces	1 piece	2	196	75	25	3	536
cut into 8 pieces	1 piece	1	171	66	22	3	469
CARRIE'S LEMON MERINGUE PIE 9" pie plate	TOTAL	175	510	440	98	30	2760
cut into 7 servings	1 piece	25	71	63	14	4	394
cut into 8 servings	1 piece	22	64	55	12	3	345
MOTHER HUBBARD SQUASH PIE 9" round pie plate	TOTAL	136	1036	144	13	33	825
cut into 7 pieces	1 piece	19	148	21	2	5	118
cut into 8 pieces	1 piece	17	130	18	1	4	103
GRANNY'S LEMON SPONGE PIE 9" pie plate	TOTAL	133	288	229	15	23	1147
cut into 7 pieces	1 piece	19	41	33	2	5	164

PUDDINGS

		Milligrams Sodium	Milligrams Potassium	Grams Carbohydrate	Grams Fat	Grams Protein	Calories
NONIE'S CUSTARD BREAD PUDDING WITH SAUCE							
5-6 servings	TOTAL	205	887	262	10	34	1273
6 servings	1 serving	34	148	44	2	5	212
BAMPY'S LEMON SNOW WITH CUSTARD SAUCE							
8 servings - no sauce	TOTAL	121	277	231	trace	26	1028
	1 serving	15	34	29	—	3	128
10 servings - no sauce	1 serving	12	28	23	—	2	103
custard sauce (approx. 1 pint)	TOTAL	23	52	14	10	22	476
BUFFY'S ORANGE-BANANA CREAM approx. 1 quart							
8 servings	TOTAL	91	1532	202	5	36	1603
	1 serving	11	192	25	1	4	125
FOAMY TAPIOCA CREME approx. 1 pint							
6 servings	TOTAL	76	71	86	5	23	481
	1 serving	12	12	14	1	4	81
EASY STEAMED CUSTARDS 7 - 5 oz custard cups							
	TOTAL	205	197	36	82	45	1062
	1 - 5 oz cup.	29	28	5	12	6	152

SALAD DRESSINGS

		Milligrams Sodium	Milligrams Potassium	Grams Carbohydrate	Grams Fat	Grams Protein	Calories
KITCHEN GARDEN DRESSING approx. 1 pint	TOTAL	64	191	217	5	8	952
HESTER'S FRENCH-STYLE DRESSING scant pint	TOTAL	29	1120	126	113	3	1528
AUNT EMMA'S BOIL-UP DRESSING approx. 1¼ cups	TOTAL	79	65	53	5	14	314
VARIATIONS FOR AUNT EMMA'S BOIL-UP DRESSING							
low-sodium catsup	1 tbls.	4					8
low-sodium chili sauce	1 tbls.	3					7

MISCELLANEOUS MARVELS

		Milligrams Sodium	Milligrams Potassium	Grams Carbohydrate	Grams Fat	Grams Protein	Calories
DEBBIE'S FILLED CREAM PUFFS 12-14 dainty puffs	TOTAL	129	183	42	57	20	757
1 unfilled puff		9					54

MISCELLANEOUS MARVELS (cont.)

		Milligrams Sodium	Milligrams Potassium	Grams Carbohydrate	Grams Fat	Grams Protein	Calories
boiled custard - medium thick	TOTAL	137	132	96	10	30	592
1 filled puff		19	23	10	5	4	89
PIQUANT MEAT SAUCE for Hamburgers or Meat Loaf	TOTAL	41	144	50	—	2	208
CINNAMON APPLE CRUNCH 6-8 servings Pan approx. 6" x 9"	TOTAL	52	1242	341	49	10	1847
1 serving - 6 to a pan		9	207	57	8	2	308
GERRY'S PANCAKES 8-12 pancakes	TOTAL	69	170	122	34	24	881
8 pancakes	1 pancake	8	21	15	4	3	111

About the Authors

ANNA HOUSTON THORBURN attended schools in Salem, Massachusetts, where she was privately tutored in piano for fifteen years. She became a music teacher, professional accompanist and ultimately played with the famous Boston Symphony's musicians' ensembles and quartets. Following hand surgery, she had to abandon her pianistic career. She became a volunteer worker at Salem Hospital, teaching First Aid throughout World War II. After the war she continued there in other capacities, eventually helping patients with salt-free menus and low sodium recipes for home cooking. Mrs. Thorburn has contributed more than ten-thousand hours as an unpaid volunteer and considers her part in this book to be a special salute to Salem Hospital's Centennial Celebration.

PHYLLIS TURNER, a graduate of Bennington College, spent seventeen years in New York City as a freelance column, article and copywriter for major magazines and newspapers. She lives with her husband, artist Hamlin Turner, in Marblehead, Massachusetts, where they raised their children. Mrs. Turner now concentrates on gardening, needlework, antiques, gourmet cooking and "at last, writing only about subjects which I feel are truly important to me and to others."

From the SIGNET Cookbook Collection

☐ **THE LOS ANGELES TIMES NATURAL FOODS COOKBOOK by Jeanne Voltz, Food Editor, Woman's Day Magazine.** Discover the joys of cooking and eating naturally with this book of over 600 savory, simple-to-follow recipes. Whether you are concerned with taste or nutrition, these delicious and healthy recipes—high in fiber content—will delight everyone from the gourmet chef to the dedicated dieter. (#E6815—$2.25)

☐ **THE JOY OF COOKING, Volume I by Irma S. Rombauer and Marion Rombauer Becker.** This all-time, bestselling cookbook is now being published in two convenient-to-use volumes. Volume I of this revised and enlarged edition contains main course recipes that will make all your meals into delicious dining. (#J5878—$1.95)

☐ **THE JOY OF COOKING, Volume II by Irma S. Rombauer and Marion Rombauer Becker.** This volume of the all-time, basic bestselling cookbook contains recipes for appetizers, desserts and baked goods that will put the finishing touch on any meal you plan. (#J5879—$1.95)

☐ **BAKE YOUR OWN BREAD and be healthier by Floss and Stan Dworkin.** Dozens of easy, delicious recipes for breads that are healthier and cheaper than "store bought" and **free of harmful additives.** This illustrated, step-by-step guide will take you through each stage of preparation for making and storing a whole bread-basket-full of old favorites and new variations. It's a simple process, easily mastered—try it!
(#Y5640—$1.25)

☐ **THE EASY WAY TO CHINESE COOKING by Beverly Lee.** In this practical, easy-to-follow guide to authentic Chinese cooking, Beverly Lee shows how to make delicious Chinese dishes—from the simplest to the most festive and elaborate. Included is a list of Chinese stores throughout the U.S. which carry the items listed in the book. (#Y6729—$1.25)

SIGNET Books for Your Reference Shelf

☐ **LET'S EAT RIGHT TO KEEP FIT by Adelle Davis.** Sensible, practical advice from America's foremost nutrition authority as to what vitamins, minerals and food balances you require; and the warning signs of diet deficiencies. (#E7245—$2.25)

☐ **EARLY DETECTION BREAST CANCER IS CURABLE by Philip Strax, M.D., Medical Director of The Guttman Breast Diagnostic Institute.** A well-known specialist tells you how you can protect yourself against the disease all women fear most. "Required reading for every woman." —American Cancer Society. (#Y6643—$1.25)

☐ **OH, MY ACHING BACK A Doctor's Guide to Your Back Pain and How to Control It by Leon Root, M.D., and Thomas Kiernan.** Introduction by James Nicholas, M.D., physician to the N.Y. Jets. Are backaches interfering with everything you do? Here is positive relief for you and tens of millions of Americans with back miseries. This wonderful, long-needed book tells you how you can free yourself of back problems—forever! (#J6512—$1.95)

☐ **WHAT EVERY PATIENT WANTS TO KNOW by Robert E. Rothenberg, M.D., F.A.C.S.** The one home medical guide that provides answers to virtually every question about your health, including surgery, heart disease, arthritis and hospital coverage, plus a complete Medicare Handbook. Here is the one book that tells you everything you need to know to protect your health and that of your loved ones. No modern home can afford to be without it. (#J6259—$1.95)